# Guidelines for Enterprise-Wide GUI Design

# Guidelines for Enterprise-Wide GUI Design

*Susan Weinschenk, Ph.D.*

*Sarah C. Yeo*

**John Wiley & Sons, Inc.**

New York • Chichester • Brisbane • Toronto • Singapore

*Dedicated to Peter, Guthrie, and Maisie*

Publisher: Katherine Schowalter
Editor: Theresa Hudson
Assistant Managing Editor: Mark Hayden
Text Design and Composition: SunCliff Graphic Productions

*This text is printed on acid-free paper.*

**Library of Congress Cataloging-in-Publication Data**

ISBN: 0-471-11845-1

Printed in the United States of America
10  9  8  7  6  5  4  3  2  1

# Contents

## Chapter 14    Customization Guide                      151

## Appendix A    List of Guidelines                       163

## Appendix B    For More Information                           177

## Appendix C    Working with the Files                          183

# Preface

A simple reason for writing this book was to answer the question I was being constantly asked by my clients, "Can you recommend one book that would have it all? One book that would contain the most important things our development teams need in order to design usable graphical user interfaces?"

It was in 1993 in Wausau, Wisconsin, however, that I was finally asked the question that would get me writing: During a one day class I was presenting on Developing and Implementing Guidelines, one of the class participants asked me how many different customized books on guidelines I had written for clients, how much of the information in each book was unique to that corporation, and how much was common across all the books. "Couldn't you," he asked, "provide a core book that would cover 80 percent of the guidelines, so that your clients would just have to customize it a little bit? Wouldn't that make the whole process faster?"

And so I began working on this book.

Interface designers, project managers, developers, and business units need a common set of look-and-feel guidelines to design and develop by. Coming up with these guidelines can be a long and difficult process, but development teams are in design and production *now*. New GUI applications can't be held up for eight months while a task force argues about guidelines. And yet without guidelines these new applications are going to have very different interfaces, and those different interfaces will make the applications hard to learn and use.

I wrote this book so that design and development teams would have guidelines in their hands now, while customized guidelines are being worked on. I wrote this book so that the process of developing customized guidelines could be sped up by starting with the 80 percent already done. And I wrote this book to finally answer the other question we get from clients, "Isn't there one book you could recommend so that I won't have to refer to many different books?"

Susan Weinschenk

# Acknowledgments

Two other people contributed to this book: John Lovgren and Sherry Kalin of Kalin and Lovgren Associates, especially the chapters on messages and metaphors. Thanks to Terri Hudson at Wiley for being interested in the book and for all her work to get it going and get it out. Thanks to Gloria Reisman for starting it all, Linda Rothenberger for keeping it all together, Wes Kranitz and Peggy Lindner for help with graphics, and Donna Kuse and Kimberly Ness for technical input. And thanks to Virginia, Guthrie, Maisie, and Peter for their patience and support.

# Introduction

## How your organization benefits from guidelines

Both users and developers can benefit from following interface design guidelines.

### How users benefit

When applications have a common look and feel they are easier to learn. Users can spend less time in training, since what they know about the last application can be applied to the new one. When applications are consistent they are more predictable. Users can worry less about how the interface is acting and concentrate more on getting their work done.

Having enterprise-wide guidelines can also help users who participate in designing new applications. Users involved with design teams know what to expect of the look and feel of the interface, and are able to concentrate on functionality. The value of their participation and feedback is enhanced.

### How developers benefit

Developers of graphical user interface (GUI) applications can benefit from using guidelines. Having guidelines to follow means some decisions have been made for you. Rather than spending time deciding where push buttons should go for each window, or what a push button should be named, developers can spend more time deciding how best to display information or perform a specific function.

Having a common set of guidelines means the developers do not have to spend time justifying every decision they make about an interface. Instead of trying to defend their decision to use certain colors, they can have the weight, research, and opinion of others with them.

## Assumptions

We make a number of assumptions in writing this book. These assumptions include:

- ❑ You are developing applications in a Windows, OS/2 or Motif environment.
- ❑ You are generally familiar with graphical user interfaces. We do not spend a lot of space describing the characteristics or workings that are common across graphical user interfaces. For example, we assume that you know what a radio button is, and have used one.

## How to use this book

You can use this book in two ways.

- ❑ You can use it as a template to customize and develop your own set of guidelines. This book can be purchased as either a stand-alone book, or with a site license to customize and distribute in your company.
- ❑ You can use it as is, right away, as a set of guidelines to follow when designing GUIs.

Use this book as a reference to look up specific topics while you are designing an application. For example, if you are working on a particular window and need to decide where to put your push buttons, go to Chapter 1, *Controls*, and look up the section for push buttons.

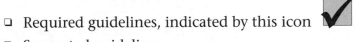

**For each topic you will find:**

- ❏ Required guidelines, indicated by this icon
- ❏ Suggested guidelines
- ❏ Examples for many of the guidelines

# *Controls*

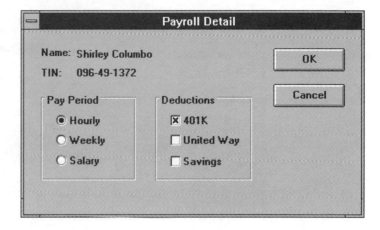

*Graphical user interfaces communicate with users through controls. The usability of your initial design depends a great deal on how you use controls.*

*This chapter discusses how to use each control to its maximum effectiveness while avoiding pitfalls.*

## Contents

# Push Buttons

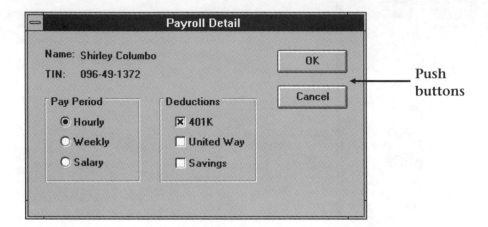

Push buttons are the primary way that users navigate from dialog box to dialog box. Use push buttons to convey to users the major actions of a particular box. Users should be able to glance at a dialog box and know what to do there and what to do next, based on the names and placement of the push buttons.

 ## Use only for frequent or critical immediate actions

Use push buttons when users are going to take immediate action that is frequent or critical. Push buttons act as reminders of what actions can and should be taken.

- ❑ Use push buttons only for actions that are frequent or critical or both.
- ❑ If an action is not frequent and not critical, place it on a pull-down menu. (See Chapter 4, *Menus*.)
- ❑ Limit push buttons to a maximum of six on a window.
- ❑ Push buttons can also appear as menu items.

Windows

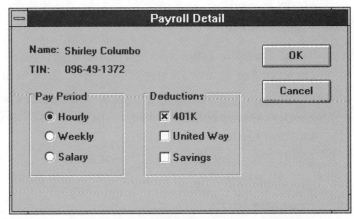

OS/2

Motif

## Label push buttons carefully

❏ Make sure the label you use for a push button is clear and concise. For example, use Print Setup, not More.

❏ Use labels with multiple words when they are needed to clearly convey the meaning of the button, for example, Print Current Orders, not Current.

❏ Capitalize only the first letter of each word in the button.

## Label consistently

Choose specific labels for certain functions and use these same labels throughout an application and from one application to another. For example, List to display a table of choices, rather than sometimes List and sometimes Search.

## Use industry standards for labels

Some labels have become standard across graphical user interfaces. Use these standard labels if you are performing the functions in the following table.

| Use this label: | To do this: | Use this mnemonic: |
| --- | --- | --- |
| OK | Makes changes and closes the window | O |
| Cancel | Does not make changes and closes the window | C |
| Close | Closes the window when changes can't be canceled | L |
| Reset | Resets to defaults, leaves window open | R |
| Apply | Makes changes, resets to defaults, leaves window open | P |
| Help | Opens online help document to particular location | H |

### Consider replacing the OK button with a specific term

If the OK push button results in a specific function such as printing
or deleting, consider using the specific term instead of the generic OK.

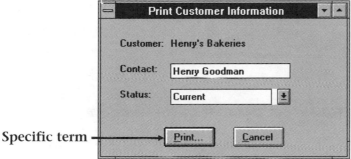

Specific term ⟶ [shown pointing to the Print... button in the dialog]

### Size buttons relative to each other

If the length of text for a series of push buttons in a dialog box is
similar, then make all the buttons on that window the size of the
largest button.

One push-
button size

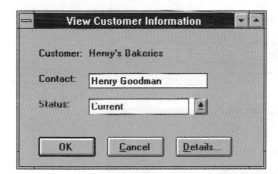

If the text length for a series of push buttons in a dialog box
varies, then use two button sizes—one for shorter text and another
for longer text.

This allows you the button size you need while avoiding too
many different sizes.

Two push-
button sizes

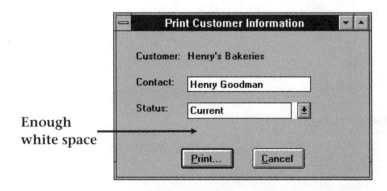

 **Separate buttons from the rest of the window**

Use white space to set off the buttons that pertain to the entire window.

Enough
white space

Not enough
white space

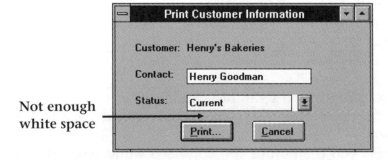

## *Group buttons together*

If you have more than three buttons, use white space to group buttons together. Group buttons to identify:

- ❑ Buttons with similar functions
- ❑ Buttons to leave the window, for example, OK and Cancel
- ❑ Destructive actions, such as Delete

White space
between
buttons

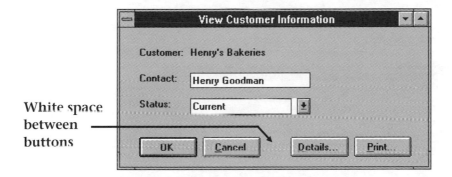

 ## *Place buttons consistently*

Use one of these locations for buttons:

- ❑ Top right of the window
- ❑ Centered on the bottom (Windows and Motif)
- ❑ Bottom left (OS/2)

Centered
buttons in
Windows

Left-aligned
buttons in
OS/2

Centered
buttons in
Motif

Top-right
buttons in
Windows

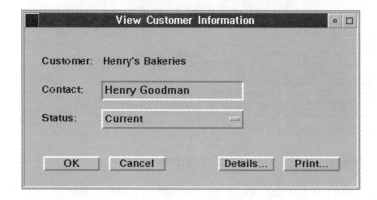

Top-right
buttons in
OS/2

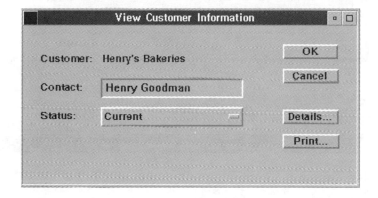

Top-right
buttons in
Motif

Do not place buttons in both bottom and right locations in one window.

## Match button position to the use of the window

Choose either a vertical design for a particular window or a horizontal design, then position the buttons to match the design:

- ❑ A horizontally designed window should have buttons on the top right.
- ❑ A vertically designed window should have buttons on the bottom.

**Horizontally designed window**

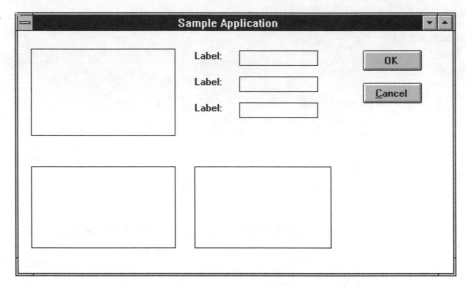

**Vertically designed window**

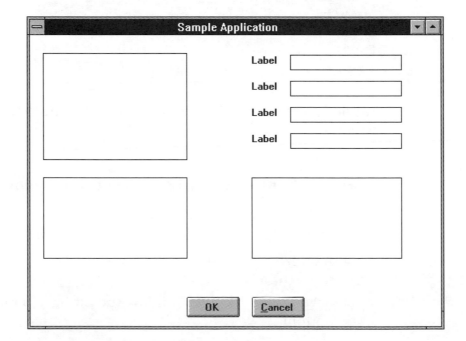

Decisions on which design to use depend on:

❑ The grouping and layout of the data in the window

❑ The length and number of buttons—if you have long button names or a lot of buttons, you may want to use a horizontal design with top right buttons

You can make these decisions on a window-by-window or box-by-box basis. Window designs do not need to be consistent across all windows or boxes.

### Position limited-action push buttons where needed

If a push button pertains only to one part of the window, place that push button where it is needed.

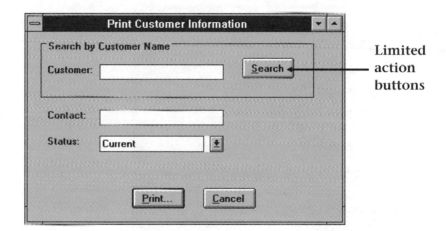

Limited action buttons

### Order buttons consistently

Whenever possible, place buttons in the following order:

1. Affirmative buttons to leave the window, for example, OK
2. Canceling actions to leave the window, for example, Cancel
3. Unique buttons for that window

This order is the same for bottom or top-right placement.

Affirmative
and Cancel-
ing buttons
come first

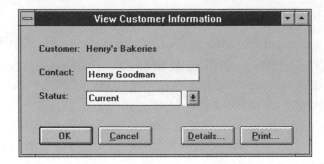

 **Use chevrons (>>) to imply an expanding dialog box**

If choosing a button results in an expanded dialog box, for example
to show additional information, use >> after the button name.

Window
before
expansion

Window
after
expansion

## Use ellipses (...) to imply an additional dialog box

If choosing a button results in a dialog box, use ellipses (...) after the button name.

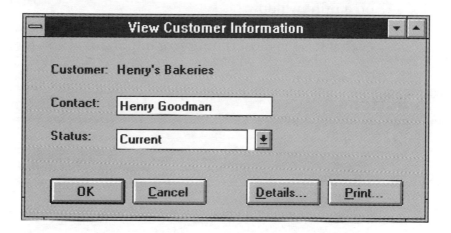

## Use graying out to show unavailability

Use graying out to show that a button's action is not available. You can use this to:

- ❑ Limit the actions allowed some users based on security.
- ❑ Restrict actions until another step is taken, for instance, requiring users to choose an item before taking the button action.

If the button will never be usable, consider not having it there at all.

**Action is available**

**Action is not available**

### Assign a nondestructive default button

Choose one button on the window as the default. If the user presses the Enter key, that button is then invoked. Make the most common or important action on that window the default, for example, Print on a print window.

Do not use a destructive button, such as Delete, as a default, even if it is the most common or important action for that window.

## Radio Buttons

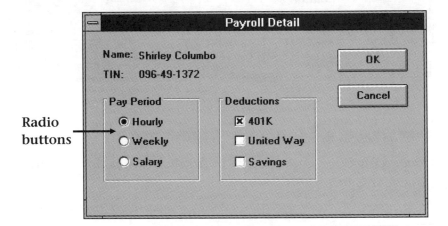

Radio buttons

### Use radio buttons for one choice

Use radio buttons when users should pick one mutually exclusive choice from a list of options, for example, choosing a pay period in a personnel application.

### Label radio buttons descriptively

Pick a clear and descriptive label for each radio button, for example, Send Course Description rather than Course.

## Group radio buttons together and label them

Place radio buttons together in a group. Use a frame to show the group. Use a descriptive label for the entire group.

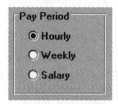

## Align radio buttons vertically

Line up radio buttons vertically rather than horizontally to make them easier to scan.

Align buttons vertically

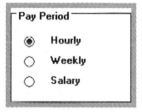

Don't align buttons horizontally

## Limit radio buttons to six or less

Limit radio buttons to six or fewer choices. If you have more choices, consider using a list box instead. List boxes are discussed later in this chapter.

### *Choose an order*

Decide on the best order for the radio buttons. Some ordering methods include:

- ❏ By frequency—most frequently used at the top
- ❏ By logic—if there is a logical order, for instance a list of dates or the order in which a task is usually performed
- ❏ By alphabet—only use alphabetical order if the labels match the way your users think about the items, use their terms and start with meaningful words

### *Avoid binary radio buttons*

If users need to make yes/no or on/off choices, use a single check box rather than radio buttons.

Do this

Don't do this

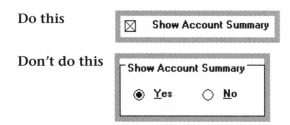

# Check Boxes

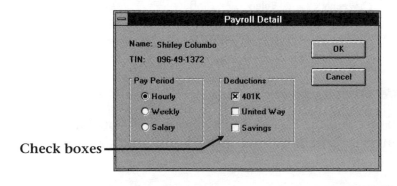

Check boxes

## Use check boxes for choosing more than one option

Use check boxes when users can choose one or more options.

 ## Use check boxes for toggling

Use check boxes when users are toggling a feature on or off. It is okay to have just one check box.

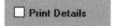

 ## Label check boxes descriptively

Pick a clear descriptive label that users will understand for each check box. For example, use Reverse Print Order, not Reverse.

## Group and label check boxes

Place check boxes together in a group. Use a frame to show the group. Use a descriptive label for the entire group.

Windows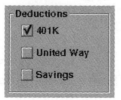

OS/2

Motif

[Deductions]
☐ 401K
☐ United Way
☐ Savings

## *Align check boxes vertically*

Line up check boxes vertically rather than horizontally to make them easier to scan.

Align
vertically

[Deductions]
☒ 401 K
☐ United Way
☐ Savings

Don't align
horizontally

[Deductions]
☒ 401 K      ☐ United Way      ☐ Savings

## *Limit check boxes to ten or fewer*

Limit check boxes to ten or fewer choices. If you have more choices consider using a multiple-select list box instead. Multiple-select list boxes are discussed later in this chapter.

## *Choose an order*

Decide on the best order for check boxes. Some ordering methods are:

- ❏ By frequency—most frequently used at the top
- ❏ By logic—if there is a logical order, for instance, a list of dates or the order in which a task is usually performed
- ❏ By alphabet—only use alphabetical order if the labels match the way your users think about the items, use their terms and start with meaningful words

## Do not use Select All or Deselect All check boxes

If you anticipate users will want to select all of a set of check boxes, or turn them all off, consider using a multiple-select list box with Select All and Deselect All buttons instead of check boxes. Multiple-select list boxes are discussed later in this chapter.

Do this

Don't do this

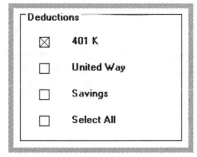

## Use check boxes in place of binary radio buttons

If users need to make yes/no or on/off choices, use a single check box rather than radio buttons.

Do this

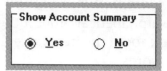

Don't do this

List Boxes
==========

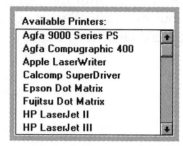

 **Use list boxes for long lists**

Use list boxes rather than radio buttons or check boxes when you have a lot of options.

| When you have...                | Use this type of list box: |
|---------------------------------|----------------------------|
| More than 6 radio button options | Single-select             |
| More than 10 check box options   | Multiple-select           |

 **Use list boxes for dynamic data**

If data is likely to change over time, use a list box rather than radio buttons or check boxes. It is easier to change the choices that appear in a list box.

## *Show three-to-eight items at a time*

Show at least three, and no more than eight, items in a list box at a time. If you have more items, use a scroll bar to view the rest of the items. See the guidelines on drop-down list boxes later in this chapter.

Windows

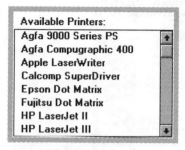

OS/2

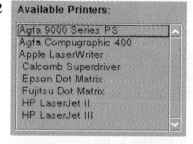

Motif

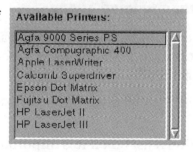

## *Label each list box*

Choose a label for the entire list box that describes the items inside the box, for example, Available Printers.

## *Use filters for large lists*

If there are more than 40 items in a list, provide a way for users to filter the list to narrow down the number of options from which they must choose.

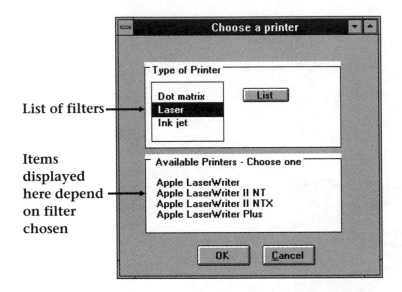

List of filters——▶

Items
displayed
here depend ——▶
on filter
chosen

## *Use drop-down list boxes to save space*

Drop-down list boxes allow you to save window space. However, they hide all but the first option from the users. Users have to go through an extra step to get to the rest of the list.

- ❑ Use a drop-down list box if most users will select the first item.
- ❑ Do not use a drop-down list box if it is important for users to see all the options all the time.
- ❑ Use a default value if you know what users will pick more than half the time.

## Use a combination list box to allow users to type in an option

A combination list box lets users type in a choice as well as pick it from the list. Use a combination list box when:

- ❏ Most users know what they want and prefer to just type it in.
- ❏ The list is long and users could skip down to a lower point in the list by typing in one or more letters.

## Use a multiple-select list box instead of check boxes

Consider using a multiple-select list box instead of check boxes if:

- ❏ You have more than ten options.
- ❏ Your list is likely to change over time.

## Consider instructions for multiple-select list boxes

Many users are not familiar with multiple-select list boxes and may not know that they can choose more than one option or may not know how to choose more than one.

Consider including a line of instruction or a prompt that tells users that they can choose more than one option. This is particularly important when one window contains both a single-select and a multiple-select list box.

Instructions give selection options

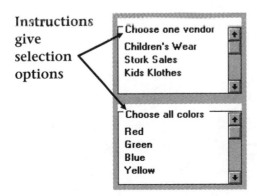

### Show pick results in a summary box

If you use a scrolling multiple-select list box, also display a box with a summary of what the user is selecting. This way, the user does not have to continually move up and down the list to see what has already been chosen.

Choice —→ 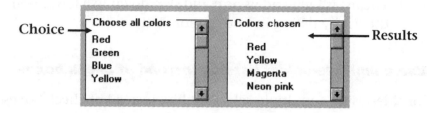 ←— Results

### Consider Select All or Deselect All buttons

If you have a set of options where you anticipate that users will want to select them all or turn them all off, consider using a multiple-select list box with Select All and Deselect All buttons rather than check boxes.

Do this

Don't do this

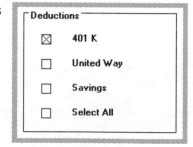

# Spin Boxes

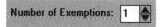

### Use spin boxes for limited cycling

Use spin boxes to cycle through possible choices when the choice list is less than ten.

### Combine spin boxes with data-entry fields

If you use spin boxes, consider combining them with data-entry fields so that users can type in the specific value they want in addition to cycling through choices.

# Sliders

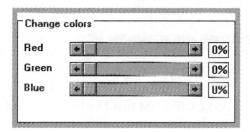

### Use sliders for visually choosing values

Consider using a slider for incrementing or decrementing continuous values. They are especially effective if you show the result.

Windows

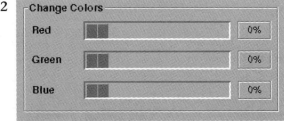

OS/2

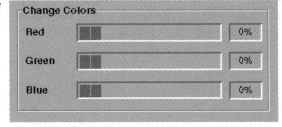

Motif

## Use sliders for large data ranges

Do not use sliders for data choices fewer than ten. For small data ranges use a different control, for instance, a spin box or a text box for data entry. Spin boxes and list boxes are discussed earlier in this chapter.

## Display results

Display the actual data value, which is equal to the slider position, as shown in the percentage boxes to the right of the slider in the example above.

### *Allow data entry*

If users know the exact value, let them enter a value directly instead of using the slider.

### *Allow the use of arrows for small increments*

Use arrows at either end of the slider for fine increments when users get close to the value they want.

## Drag and Drop

### *Consider drag-and-drop interaction*

When users have to sort objects into categories, or select more than one object, consider using a drag-and-drop interaction. An example is having users click on and drag particular documents into one box for printing and a different box for deleting.

### *Avoid a single use of drag-and-drop*

If you use drag and drop, you should try to make it a frequent interaction. Avoid using it just in one place in your application because it is then just a distraction. Users will quickly adjust to drag and drop if it is used frequently.

### *Use visual feedback*

Use visual feedback for drag-and-drop interactions, making sure that users can see the results of the dragging immediately, and that the results stay visible while the task is being completed.

## List of Guidelines for Controls

### Push Buttons

Use only for frequent or critical immediate actions
Label push buttons carefully
Label consistently
Use industry standards for labels
Consider replacing the OK button with a specific term
Size buttons relative to each other
Separate buttons from the rest of the window
Group buttons together
Place buttons consistently
Match button position to the use of the window
Position limited-action push buttons where needed
Order buttons consistently
Use chevrons (>>) to imply an expanding dialog box
Use ellipses (...) to imply an additional dialog box
Use graying out to show unavailability
Assign a nondestructive default button

### Radio Buttons

Use radio buttons for one choice
Label radio buttons descriptively
Group radio buttons together and label them
Align radio buttons vertically
Limit radio buttons to six or less
Choose an order
Avoid binary radio buttons

### Check Boxes

Use check boxes for choosing more than one option
Use check boxes for toggling
Label check boxes descriptively
Group and label check boxes

Align check boxes vertically
Limit check boxes to ten or fewer
Choose an order
Do not use Select All or Deselect All check boxes
Use check boxes in place of binary radio buttons

## List Boxes

Use list boxes for long lists
Use list boxes for dynamic data
Show three to eight items at a time
Label each list box
Use filters for large lists
Use drop-down list boxes to save space
Use a combination list box to allow users to type in an option
Use a multiple-select list box instead of check boxes
Consider instructions for multiple-select list boxes
Show pick results in a summary box
Consider Select All or Deselect All buttons

## Spin Boxes

Use spin boxes for limited cycling
Combine spin boxes with data-entry fields

## Sliders

Use sliders for visually choosing values
Use sliders for large data ranges
Display results
Allow data entry
Allow the use of arrows for small increments

## Drag and Drop

Consider drag-and-drop interaction
Avoid a single use of drag and drop
Use visual feedback

# Data Fields

```
┌─────────────────────────────────────┐
│ ─        Client Data                │
├─────────────────────────────────────┤
│  Name:     │Jerry Siegel        │    │
│  Address:  │34 W. 22nd St.      │    │
│            │Milwaukee, WI 53202 │    │
│  Phone:    │(414) 392-5566      │    │
│  Spouse:   │Amy                 │    │
│  Employer: │Northern Electric   │    │
│                                     │
│    ┌───────────┐   ┌───────────┐   │
│    │    OK     │   │  Cancel   │   │
│    └───────────┘   └───────────┘   │
└─────────────────────────────────────┘
```

*One of the most important functions of a GUI window is to present or enter data. This chapter includes guidelines on how to use graphical user interfaces to convey or enter data.*

## Contents

## Presenting and Entering Data

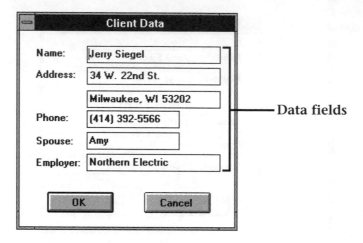

Data fields

 ### *Place a box around data-entry fields*

Enclose data-entry fields in a box.

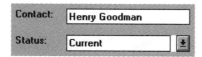

 ### *Show display-only data without a box*

If data is display only and cannot be changed or added, do not use a box around it.

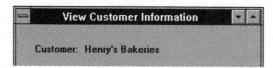

## Use graying out for temporarily protected fields

If a particular field is temporarily protected, gray out the box around it to signify that data cannot be entered or changed *at this time*.

Employer: [              ] ◄───── Available

Employer: [              ] ◄───── Temporarily protected and unavailable

## Use the box length to signify data length

Size data-entry boxes to indicate the approximate length of the field.

## Match the lengths of data boxes

If you have data boxes of similar length, make them the same length.

| Name: | Jerry Siegel |
|-------|--------------|
| Address: | 34 W. 22nd St. |
|  | Milwaukee, WI 53202 |

## Align data fields

Left-align data fields on the screen to minimize the number of different margins.

Windows

OS/2

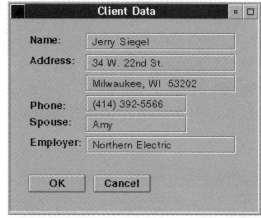

Motif

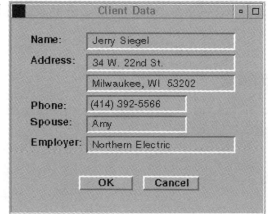

### Group data fields

If you have data fields that all pertain to similar information, group them together in a frame and label the entire group.

## Data-Field Labels

Data-
field
labels

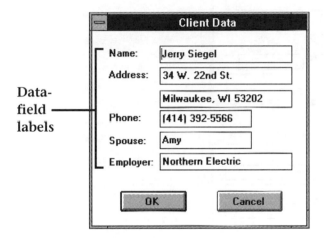

### Label all data fields

Assign a descriptive label to every data field. Avoid acronyms or abbreviations unless you are sure all users will understand them.

### Place labels to the left

Place labels for data-entry fields to the left of the field. Avoid placing labels on top of data-entry fields.

## *Align data-entry labels to the left*

Align data-entry labels on the left. Avoid ragged left margins.

Left-align
labels

**Vendor Information**

Name:
Street:
City:
State:
Zip:
Phone:
Contact:

Don't right-
align labels

**Vendor Information**

Name:
Street:
City:
State:
Zip:
Phone:
Contact:

## *Place a colon after data labels*

Use a colon after data labels to distinguish between the label and
the data that follows. Do not use colons after group frame names
or column headings.

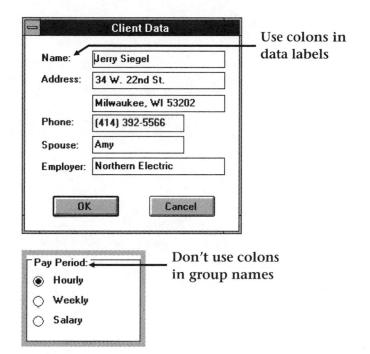

Use colons in
data labels

Don't use colons
in group names

## List of Guidelines for Data Fields

### Presenting and Entering Data

Place a box around data-entry fields
Show display-only data without a box
Use a graying out for temporarily protected fields
Use the box length to signify data length
Match the lengths of data boxes
Align data fields
Group data fields

### Data-Field Labels

Label all data fields
Place labels to the left
Align data-entry labels to the left
Place a colon after data labels

# Chapter 3

# Dialog Boxes and Windows

```
┌─────────────────────────────────┐
│ ─        Client Data            │
├─────────────────────────────────┤
│ Name:      │Jerry Siegel        │
│ Address:   │34 W. 22nd St.      │
│            │Milwaukee, WI 53202 │
│ Phone:     │(414) 392-5566      │
│ Spouse:    │Amy                 │
│ Employer:  │Northern Electric   │
└────────┌─────────────────────────────────┐
         │ ─        Employer Details       │
         ├─────────────────────────────────┤
         │ Supervisor:  │                │ │
         │ Address:     │                │ │
         │              │                │ │
         │     [   OK   ]     [  Cancel  ] │
         └─────────────────────────────────┘
```

*Instead of full screens, the major units of work in graphical user interfaces are dialog boxes and windows. This chapter focuses on using dialog boxes and windows effectively.*

## Contents

## Presentation of Windows and Dialog Boxes

### *Use cascading windows*

Use cascading windows unless you have a strong reason to tile them. For example, if by cascading you would be covering up information that needs to be viewed simultaneously, use tiling.

Cascading
windows

Tiled
windows

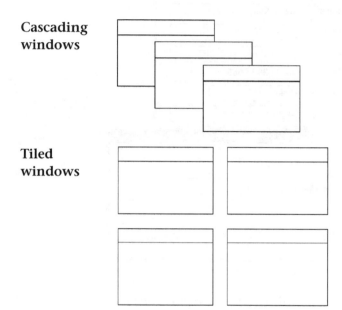

Tiling windows allows users to see all the information at once. However, you cannot display very many windows.

Cascading windows may cover some of the information contained in the previous window, but they keep users focused on one task at a time.

### *Avoid horizontal scrolling*

Avoid having users scroll horizontally to see information in a window or dialog box. Instead of horizontal scrolling, try one or more of the following:

❑ A larger window

❑ Breaking the information up into more than one window

❑ Allow expanding, zooming in, and collapsing to show only some information at a time

## Use expanding dialogs

Use expanding dialogs in place of some cascading windows.

When users choose to expand a dialog box, the box seems to grow, rather than being overlapped by another window.

Before
expansion

After
expansion

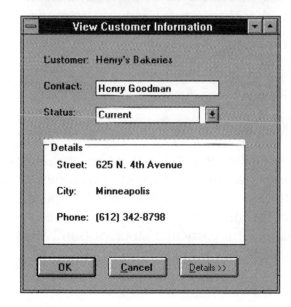

From the users' point of view, more information has appeared, rather than the box being covered over or replaced with another one. Using expanding dialogs helps alleviate the feeling that the interface is chopped up into many small pieces.

### Size secondary windows to fit data

Size secondary windows and dialogs to best fit the information in them. Do not rely on users to resize windows, even if the window allows it. All secondary windows *do not* have to be the same size.

### Place pop-ups in the center of the action

Place pop-up windows and dialogs in the center of the area they relate to in the application window.

### Use modal dialogs for closure

A modal dialog box must be responded to before work can be performed in any other box or window. Use modal dialog boxes:

- ❑ For form filling
- ❑ For small, discrete tasks

### Use modeless dialogs for continuing work

A modeless dialog box is a dialog that can remain open and active even while users perform work in other windows or dialogs. Use a modeless dialog box for tasks that need to be repeated or monitored over time. For example, use a modeless dialog box for monitoring the performance of a particular stock or bond within Wall Street trading software.

## Navigation and Order

### *Organize windows and dialogs to match work flow*

What windows you have, how much they do, and the order they are in, should match how the users are doing their work.

### *Use an appropriate amount of information*

Each window or dialog should represent one task or subtask in the user's work flow. If a task is complicated, use more than one window—one for each subtask.

### *Find a home*

The home is the screen or window users come back to again and again while working on a particular task.

Decide on a window that will serve as the users' home. The home might be a screen of data, a list, or a form with or without data. Home is not necessarily the first window they see when they enter the application or a particular task. Users might go through a series of selection and list screens before reaching home.

Do not make home a blank screen with a menu bar. It should be a screen with meaningful information for the task they are performing; for example, a list of contracts or a blank invoice form.

Having a home helps users remember what to do, gives them a concrete and visual anchor point, and helps alleviate the feeling of being lost in the interface.

### *Organize information within a window*

Information should be placed in a window or dialog box so that it flows well with the task the users have to perform. The most common or critical information should be at the top left of the window or dialog. The flow of the window should then move from top to bottom or left to right.

### Choose a horizontal or vertical flow

Decide whether you will use a horizontal or a vertical flow of information for each window or dialog.

**Horizontal flow**

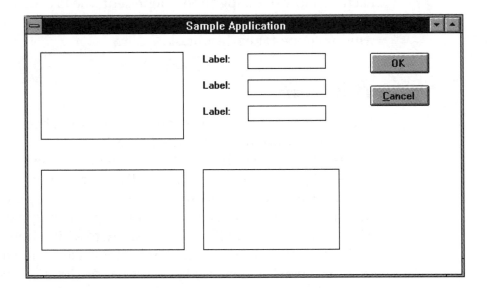

- ❑ A horizontal flow starts in the upper left and moves to the right.
- ❑ The most common or critical information appears in the top row. Less common or critical information appears in a second row.
- ❑ Buttons to control the window are on the top right.
- ❑ Use white space between rows to show the horizontal flow.

## Vertical flow

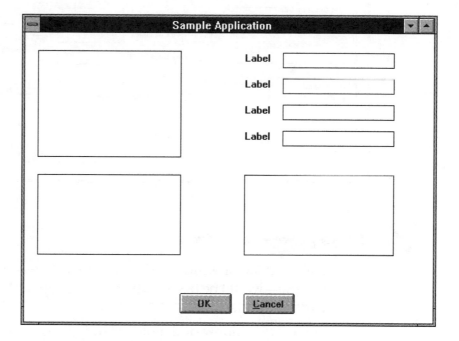

- ❏ A vertical flow starts in the upper left and moves down.
- ❏ The most common or critical information appears in the left column. Less common or critical information appears in a second column.
- ❏ Buttons to control the window are centered on the bottom.
- ❏ Use white space between columns to show the vertical flow.

 ### Group similar data

Group data together. Use frames and white space to show the groupings. Label the groups.

 ### Minimize different margins

Line up data elements and groups to minimize the number of different margins on the screen.

Too many
margins

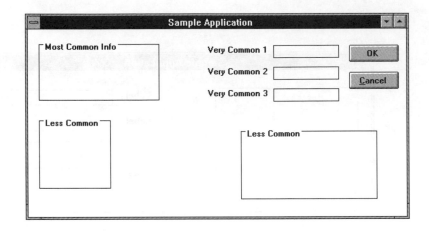

## *Some general guidelines*

❑ For a particular window, choose which flow—horizontal or vertical—would be best for the information in that particular window or dialog.

❑ Not every window or dialog has to have the same flow—decide separately for each window or dialog box.

❑ Make sure you show the flow with white space and the placement of buttons. Avoid confused flows where it is not obvious which way the screen is designed.

See Chapter 1, *Controls*, for more information on placing buttons.

## List of Guidelines for Dialog Boxes and Windows

### Presentation of Windows and Dialog Boxes

Use cascading windows
Avoid horizontal scrolling
Use expanding dialogs
Size secondary windows to fit data
Place pop-ups in the center of the action

Use modal dialogs for closure

Use modeless dialogs for continuing work

## Navigation and Order

Organize windows and dialogs to match work flow

Use an appropriate amount of information

Find a home

Organize information within a window

Choose a horizontal or vertical flow

Group similar data

Minimize different margins

Some general guidelines

# *Menus*

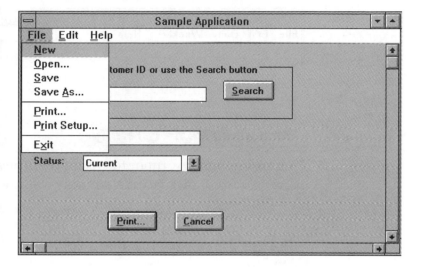

*Menus play two critical roles in graphical user interfaces. They are a major form of navigation through the interface and they convey the mental model to the user in a snapshot. Giving attention to the design of usable menus is time well spent.*

## Contents

## Designing Effective Menus

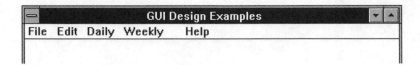

 ### Word menu items carefully

Pick names and test them to ensure that they make sense to users. It is not easy to pick labels that users will understand.

### Change menus as you need to

It is okay for menu bars and their pull-downs to change as users move through an application.

### Use initial caps

Menu-bar items should have an initial capital letter with the rest of the word in lower case.

Start each pull-down item with a capital letter, leaving the rest of the letters lower case.

 ### Follow industry standards

Follow industry standards on menu bars and pull-down menus. You do not have to use these menu-bar items or their pull-downs if you do not have these tasks in your menu.

File menu
for Windows

File menu
for OS/2

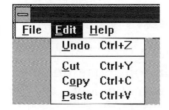

Edit menu
for Windows

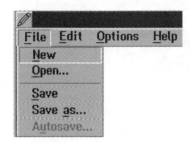

Edit menu
for OS/2

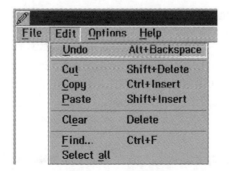

Help menu
for Windows

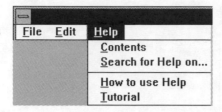

Help menu
for OS/2

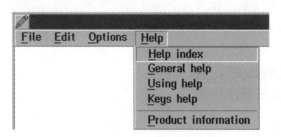

## Menu Bars

 ### *Match menu bars to the users' work flow*

When users look at a menu bar it should match how they think of their work. Spend time deciding on and testing menu categories to make sure they fit the users' mental model.

### *Give critical or frequent tasks even weight*

Make sure all critical or frequent tasks are represented equally on the menu bar. Avoid grouping all critical or frequent items under one category, and then using the remaining five or six items on the menu bar for different, but nonessential, tasks.

### *Place application-specific menu items where they fit*

Place menu-bar items that are specific to your application where they best fit, for example, Jobs and Preferences before Help.

### *Replace the word File if necessary*

If you have file activities, such as opening, closing, saving, or printing, you can opt to use an application-specific word in place of the word File, such as Contracts.

Consider, however, using the standard word File. If users are familiar with GUI applications they will look for the word File. Only use a more specific word if you are sure you have users who will not know what File means.

### *Use one word only for menu-bar items*

Items on the menu bar must be one word only. If they are more than one word, or use hyphens or dashes, it is hard to tell whether they are one item or two.

Don't use two
words as one
menu item ——————

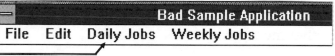

### *Use only one line for the menu bar*

Menu bars must be only one line long. If you have too many items on your menu bar for one line, then collapse some of your items into one.

Don't do

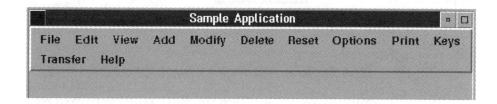

### Do not gray out menu bar items

Do not use graying out to make menu bar items temporarily unavailable. Instead you should do one of the following:

❏ Change the menu bar and do not show that item at all.

❏ Remove the item from the menu bar, collapse categories, and put it into a pull-down. Then you can gray it out since it will be a pull-down item, not a menu bar item.

## Pull-Downs

### Use more than one pull-down item

Pull-down menus should have more than one item on them. If you have a menu-bar item that has one or no pull-down items, then it should not be a separate menu-bar category. Combine it with another menu item.

### Use unique pull-down items

Do not start each pull-down item with the same word that is on the menu bar. Pull-down items should be unique.

Don't repeat menu name in pull-down

### Use up to one screen length of pull-downs

Pull-downs can go from the top to the bottom of the screen. Do not use scrolling. If you have more items than will fit on the screen, you will need to combine some and use cascading pull-downs, or separate some into an additional menu-bar item.

### Put frequent or important items at the top

Place the most frequent or critical items at the top of the pull-down menu.

### Use separator bars

Use separator bars in pull-down menus in two ways:

1. To group related items
2. To separate destructive items

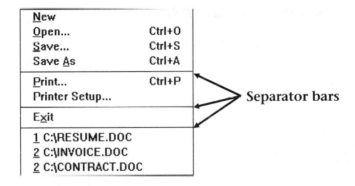

### Use no more than two levels of cascading

It is okay to use cascading pull-down menus, but do not use more than two levels of cascading. Use    to denote that a pull-down item contains a cascading menu.

Avoid too many cascading pull-down menus

## Use ellipses (...) to denote dialogs

Use ellipses (...) after a pull-down item to denote that that item will result in a dialog box rather than immediate action.

## Use industry-standard keyboard equivalents

A keyboard equivalent allows users to choose a menu item without using the mouse. A keyboard equivalent requires that the pull-down be open when it is used.

Keyboard equivalent

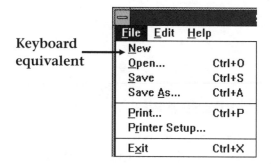

## Use accelerators sparingly

Accelerators are combinations of keystrokes that allow users to choose a menu item when the pull-down is not open. Use accelerators only for those pull-down menu items that you think users will

want to use without pulling down a menu, for example, Ctrl-V to
paste from the clipboard.

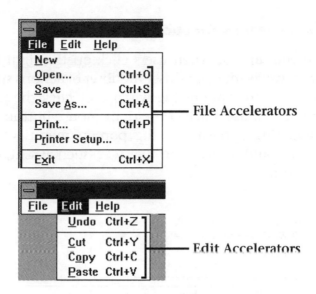

File Accelerators

Edit Accelerators

 **Use consistent accelerators**

Use consistent accelerators across your enterprise-wide applications. Place the accelerators in the pull-down menus, to the right
of the pull-down menu option.

OS/2 uses different accelerators. If you are primarily using OS/2
in your enterprise-wide applications, you may want to match the
OS/2 standard accelerators.

OS/2
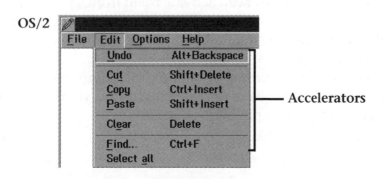

Accelerators

## Special Menus

### *Use pop-up menus for specific options*

Pop-up menus appear when users click on the right button. Use them when you want to give users a subset of actions specific to the place or action they are taking when they click the right button. For example, if a user clicked the right-mouse button on text in a word processing application, the pop-up menu would contain actions that could be taken on that text, such as Cut, Copy, Paste, and Formatting.

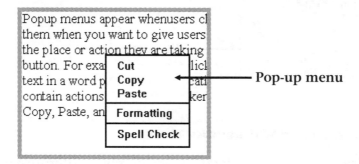

Pop-up menu

### *Consider using roll-up menus*

Roll-up menus are floating, or movable, menus. They have a similar feel to toolbars. The user can activate them from a pull-down menu and place them anywhere in the workspace. By clicking the top-right corner, the user can cause them to roll down (expand) or contract (roll up).

Use these for a group of actions that users will go back to frequently until they have the exact result they want, like applying special effects in a graphics application.

Roll-up
menu
rolled up

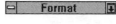

Roll-up
menu
unrolled

## List of Guidelines for Menus

### Designing Effective Menus

Word menu items carefully

Change menus as you need to

Use initial caps

Follow industry standards

### Menu Bars

Match menu bars to the users' work flow

Give critical or frequent tasks even weight

Place application-specific menu items where they fit

Replace the word File if necessary

Use one word only for menu-bar items

Use only one line for the menus

Do not gray out menu-bar items

### Pull-Downs

Use more than one pull-down item

Use unique pull-down items

Use up to one screen length of pull-downs

Put frequent or important items at the top

Use separator bars

Use no more than two levels of cascading

Use ellipses (...) to denote dialogs

Use industry-standard keyboard equivalents

Use accelerators sparingly

Use consistent accelerators

## Special Menus

Use pop-up menus for specific options

Consider using roll-up menus

# *Messages*

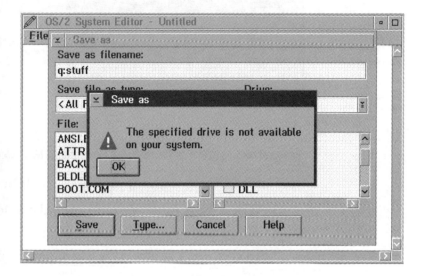

*Messages are how we communicate with users from within a graphical user interface. Users often judge the usability of a GUI from its ability to communicate with messages.*

## Contents

## Presenting Messages

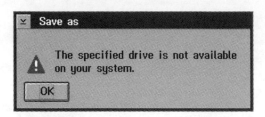

### *Use messages when and where they are needed*

Give users messages and feedback in the following situations:

- ❏ When users must respond or make a decision
- ❏ When users must correct data entry
- ❏ To confirm a destructive action, such as deleting
- ❏ When processing will take longer than five seconds
- ❏ When processing will take longer than users might expect

Remember, users often decide on the friendliness of your interface based on the quantity and quality of your messages. This is not just a nice touch. Good messages at the right times are an essential component of user-friendly software.

### *Place messages in the center of the current activity*

Put messages where they will be noticed—usually in the center of the current window or dialog box. Avoid message lines at the bottom of the screen except for one-line micro help used for data-input hints or messages.

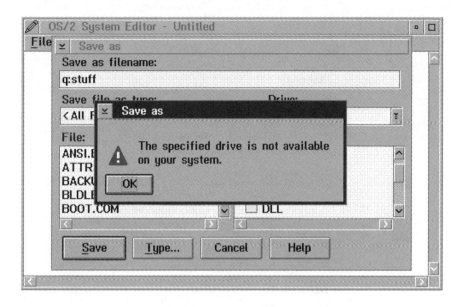

## Wording

### Be descriptive

You now have a window to use for your message rather than just part of a single line. Use this space to say what you need.

- ❏ Put the most important information at the beginning of the message.
- ❏ Avoid using OK.
- ❏ Use Yes, No, and Cancel buttons to answer a question in a message. OK, instead of Yes and No, can be confusing when answering questions.

### Use active voice

Use active voice rather than passive voice for messages. Users respond more quickly and accurately to active voice.

**Passive voice:**

The form will be completed.

**Active voice:**

You will complete the form.
The system will complete the form.
Have your supervisor complete the form.
Complete the form.

### Use terms the users understand

Use terminology and wording that users will understand:

- ❏ Make sure you are not using any unfamiliar technical terms.
- ❏ Use short words as much as possible.
- ❏ Avoid codes, acronyms, and abbreviations unless you are sure all users will understand them.

### Avoid humor and humanizing

Do not use humor in messages. It is easy for users to take the humor the wrong way, especially when they are frustrated or trying to recover from an error.

Resist the temptation to make the computer seem human, for example, using I, He, or She.

Do not let *your* frustration come through in the message.

## Different Message Types

### Use information messages for results

Use an information message to tell users the results of their actions or requests. Provide an OK button to close the message window.

In Windows and OS/2 the information symbol is a white lower-case *i* in a blue circle.

Windows

OS/2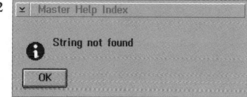

In Motif this symbol is a gray lower-case *i*.

Motif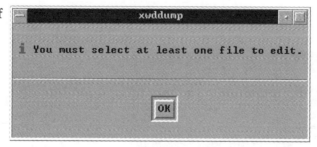

## Use warning messages for critical confirmations

Use warning messages when users may destroy data or do something that will have irreversible consequences. Provide Yes, No, and Cancel buttons.

In Windows, this symbol is a black exclamation point inside a yellow circle.

Windows

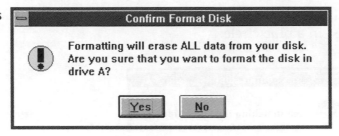

In OS/2, this symbol is a white exclamation point inside a green triangle.

OS/2

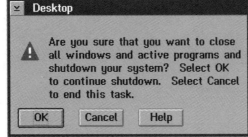

In Motif, this symbol is a gray exclamation point.

Motif

## Use critical messages for system errors

Use critical messages when there is a serious system or application error that is not a result of user action. These messages are often generated by the operating system. Require users to press the OK button to make sure they have seen the message.

Use the ⬣ or ⊘ symbol for critical messages, depending on your platform. In Windows, the symbol is a red stop sign. In OS/2, it is a red circle with a diagonal line.

Windows

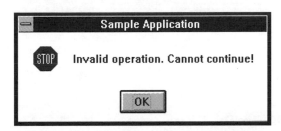

OS/2

### Use in-progress messages for waits

Show an in-progress or feedback message whenever the user has to wait more than five seconds for processing, or when processing a request will take longer than the user is accustomed to waiting.

## Error Messages

### Use three critical pieces of information

Each error message should have three pieces of information:

1. What the user did
2. Why it was not correct
3. What to do to correct it

Tell users the steps necessary to recover. Do not just announce that there is a problem.

| | |
|---|---|
| **Contains critical pieces** | You entered a start date later than the end date. The start date must be earlier than the end date. Check the dates and re-enter. |
| **Missing critical pieces** | Invalid dates. |

## Don't blame users

Tell the users what happened without blaming them. Do not write messages that are hostile, blaming, or threatening. Do not imply that they made a mistake.

## Use Help on error messages

Consider having a Help button on the error message and providing context-sensitive help as to how to recover from the problem. See Chapter 13, Online Help, for more information.

## Avoid negative wording

Tell users what they did and what they should do rather than what they didn't do, or what they shouldn't.

| | |
|---|---|
| **Positive wording** | The start date must be an earlier date than the end date. |
| **Negative wording** | Do not enter a start date that is later than the end date. |

# Feedback and In-Progress Messages

## *Use two critical pieces of information for feedback*

Each feedback message should state:

1. What the computer has done
2. Whether it was successful

## *Inform users how long the wait will be*

For in-progress messages, let users know how long they must wait in terms of time, transactions processed, or percentage complete.

## *Show progress status visually*

For in-progress messages, show users how long the wait will be with an animation indicating the computer is working on the request and what its status is. This can be done with a bar that fills in, dots being drawn on the screen, or a similar graphic.

# List of Guidelines for Messages

### Presenting Messages

Use messages when and where they are needed
Place messages in the center of the current activity

### Wording

Be descriptive
Use active voice
Use terms the users understand
Avoid humor and humanizing

### Different Message Types

Use information messages for results
Use warning messages for critical confirmations
Use critical messages for system errors
Use in-progress messages for waits

### Error Messages

Use three critical pieces of information
Don't blame users
Use Help on error messages
Avoid negative wording

### Feedback and In-Progress Messages

Use two critical pieces of information for feedback
Inform users how long the wait will be
Show progress status visually

# Color

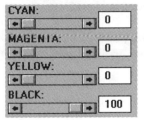

You now have the capability of using color in your
interfaces. Often, however, color decisions distract users
rather than enhancing usability. This chapter discusses
how to use color effectively.

**Chapter 6**

## Contents

## Using Color

### Use color to get attention

Putting something in a different color on a screen is attention-getting. Use color when it is critical that users notice a certain part of the screen.

### Use color sparingly

Color is a powerful attention-getting technique. Use it sparingly or it loses its effectiveness. Do not use it only for aesthetic purposes. Every time you use color it should be for a specific, attention-getting reason.

### Limit colors to three per screen

Outside of black, white, and gray, use no more than three colors on a screen. Using only one or two colors per screen is preferable.

### Combine color with redundant highlighting

Because you cannot rely on users' recognizing a particular color—some people have impaired color perception, users can change their color palettes—combine color with redundant highlighting. For example, make a part of the screen blue *and* bold.

### Watch out for color blindness

Nine percent of men and two percent of women have some form of color blindness or color confusion. Do not rely on color alone to provide critical cues.

### Watch out for color customizing

People can often change their color palettes. Do not refer to parts of the screen by specific color, for instance, "Enter data that is required into the green box." You cannot be sure that the box is still green.

### Consider the restrictions of monochrome monitors

Some people, such as laptop users, use monochrome monitors. Make sure you use redundant highlighting so that monochrome users can make critical distinctions.

 ### Use colors consistently

Decide on the specific meanings of colors and use them and their redundant highlighting consistently.

### Use color in icons sparingly

Because of their small size, using color in icons (bitmap images) is often more of a distraction than it is useful. Use color in icons only for:

- ❑ Distinguishing certain aspects of the icon (for example, different colors for different bars on a bar-chart icon)
- ❑ Particular meaning (red in a stop sign)

## Color Choices and Combinations

 ### Follow cultural color meanings

Be aware of the cultural meanings colors have for your particular users and follow them. In the United States, for example, some colors have particular meanings:

| Color | Means |
|-------|-------|
| Red | Danger, Stop, Hot, or Financial Loss |
| Yellow | Warning or Caution |
| Green | Go or OK |
| Blue | Cool |
| Black | Financial Profit |

Do not violate these meanings and make sure you follow any additional meanings your users have. Be aware of international color associations—they vary from culture to culture.

### Use light backgrounds for main areas

The best colors to use for screen and window backgrounds are off-whites and light grays. If you need to use a color for a background, use a pale yellow or pale blue.

### Avoid red-and-blue combinations

Red and blue together, either as background/foreground or in adjacent areas, is very hard on the eyes.

### Avoid deep blue for backgrounds

Do not use a deep saturated blue for the backgrounds of screens or windows that are used for more than five minutes. This color is very hard on the eyes.

### Avoid blue text

Recent research shows that blue text recedes or fades away. Use black for text on a screen.

### Use enough contrast

Choose colors for your background and foreground (text or data) that have enough contrast between them. For example, do not use a light-blue background with medium-blue text on it.

### Avoid light text on dark

Avoid using light-colored text on a dark background. This combination appears to blur. It is better to use light-colored backgrounds with dark foregrounds. For example, use a light-gray background with black text.

 ### Use grayware first

The best colors to use for backgrounds and foregrounds are black, white, and shades of gray. Although developers often consider this boring, it is best for users over the long run. Save color for when you really need to get someone's attention. Different shades of gray can be very effective in delineating areas on a screen.

Design in grayware first, adding color as needed.

## Color in Graphs and Charts

### Use primary colors to show differences

Use primary colors like green, blue, and yellow in charts and graphs to make sharp distinctions. For example, use a different color for each bar in a bar chart or each slice in a pie chart.

### Avoid red

Avoid using red in a chart or graph unless you mean to imply trouble, danger, or stop.

### *Use close colors to show transition*

Use colors that are close to each other like medium and light blue to show a transition; for example, sales increasing step by step from month to month.

### *Use light backgrounds for tables*

Use off-white or light gray as the background for data in a table. Use black text for the foreground. Use color only when you need to highlight a particular cell, row, or column.

## User Customizing

### *Let users customize*

It is okay to let users customize their colors, but do not use this as a reason for not choosing good color combinations. Users should not have to customize their screen appearance just because you picked poor colors.

### *Use color palettes*

Provide a few color palette choices for users. This enables them to change all the colors quickly, and ensures that general principles for color use are not violated.

### *Provide a reset*

If you let users customize colors, make sure you have an obvious and easy way for them to return to the original (default) colors.

### Show results before setting

Show users the results of their color decisions *before* they finally apply them. You can do this by providing a preview function in which they can see the color changes on a small sample screen before finishing the color dialog.

## List of Guidelines for Color

### Using Color

Use color to get attention

Use color sparingly

Limit colors to three per screen

Combine color with redundant highlighting

Watch out for color blindness

Watch out for color customizing

Consider the restrictions of monochrome monitors

Use colors consistently

Use color in icons sparingly

### Color Choices and Combinations

Follow cultural color meanings

Use light backgrounds for main areas

Avoid red-and-blue combinations

Avoid deep blue for backgrounds

Avoid blue text

Use enough contrast

Avoid light text on dark

Use grayware first

### Color in Graphs and Charts

Use primary colors to show differences

Avoid red

Use close colors to show transition
Use light backgrounds for tables

## User Customizing

Let users customize
Use color palettes
Provide a reset
Show results before setting

# Icons and Toolbars

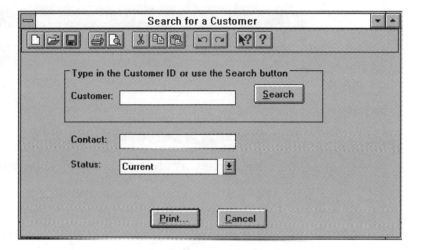

*A picture is worth a thousand words—if it is the right picture and users can see and interpret it. This chapter summarizes the dos and don'ts of using icons as application launchers and button images, and using toolbars: collections of button images that allow quick and easy access to frequently used commands and choices.*

## Contents

## When to Use Icons

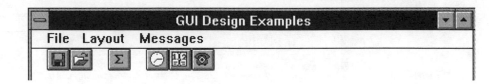

### *Use icons for a purpose*

There are three ways to use icons, or small images, in software:

**Application icons.**  These usually appear on the desktop. Clicking them launches the application.

**Button images.**  These are simple pictures that are placed on buttons, usually grouped together on a toolbar. Clicking them starts an action in the application, such as printing.

**Message icons.**  These are symbols, often used in messages, that quickly communicate the message's importance and general purpose, for example, information and warnings.

Decide how an image will be used before designing or choosing the image itself.

### *Use button images as shortcuts*

Use pictures on push buttons when you want users to be able to find critical or frequently used objects or actions without searching through menus.

### *Use icons when a picture is worth . . .*

Some ideas are best and most quickly portrayed with a picture rather than words—for instance, drawing tools.

## Use icons for international use

If you are designing for international and multilanguage audiences, consider using pictures to eliminate the need to translate words.

# Designing or Choosing Pictures

## Decide on an approach

When designing a set of icons you can use one of several different approaches:

| Approach | Example of Approach | Example Icons* |
|----------|---------------------|----------------|
| Object | A picture of a disk to represent an actual disk | 💾 |
| Action | A picture of someone running to indicate speed | 🏃 |
| Tool that represents the action | A ruler to indicate measuring | 📏 |
| The result | Showing italicized text | *Result* |
| Physical analogy | Magnifying glass to show enlargement or zooming in | 🔍 |
| Commonly used symbol | International "Don't do" symbol | 🚫 |
| Letter | The letter "i" for information | i |

*All pictures in this example are from *The Icon Book and Disk: Visual Symbols for Computer Systems and Documentation* by William Horton (John Wiley & Sons, 1994).

### Develop a cohesive set

Develop sets or families of icons using the same approach described previously.

- ❑ Your entire set of icons for the whole application may involve several sets or families.
- ❑ Keep the number of different subsets to a minimum.

**Example:**

For editing a document, you could use tools that represent an action, such as scissors for cutting or a magnifying glass for enlarging.

### Include just enough detail for recognition

If you are designing your own icons, use just enough detail so that people can recognize the picture. Avoid using too much detail and having the picture look like a photograph.

### Use standard pictures

If possible, use standard icons that have already been tested. A good source is: *The Icon Book and Disk: Visual Symbols for Computer Systems and Documentation* by William Horton (John Wiley & Sons, 1994).

### Consider changing the button image's state

Consider having a button image change to represent a new idea. For example, a closed file folder representing a file, which then changes to an open file folder representing an open file.

### Test your images

Make sure you test the images you design or choose. There are two basic ways to test:

❑ Give users a particular task and ask them to pick the icon they believe performs the task.

❑ Give users icons in context and ask them what actions the icons represent.

## Using Pictures in the Interface

### *Be consistent*

Once you have chosen or designed an image, use it consistently. For example, do not use different representations of a phone in different parts of the application.

### *Avoid words*

A well-designed button image should not need a label. If you do use labels, here are your placement choices:

1. Use bubble labels. If possible have the bubble label appear when the cursor passes over the icon.
2. Use a label underneath the picture.
3. Use a label in micro-help (line at the bottom of the screen). Use this only if you cannot use either of the above choices.

If users can't decipher the pictures, you may need to fix the pictures rather than just adding words.

### *Watch out for international meanings*

If you are using icons with international audiences, make sure that:

❑ They are widely understood. Test them with different groups.

❑ You do not use any offensive gestures. For example, a pointing finger is considered offensive in some cultures.

❑ Your representations are universally held. For example, scales to show balancing is not a universal representation.

## Toolbars

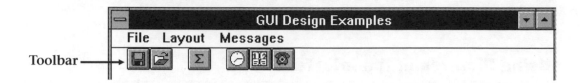

Toolbar

### Use toolbars for frequent actions across screens

Toolbars should contain actions that users need to take fairly often and across several screens. Do *not* use toolbars instead of word push buttons.

| Put these actions | Here... |
|---|---|
| Most frequent and critical | Word push buttons |
| Fairly frequent and across several screens | Toolbar |
| All actions, frequent, critical, and infrequent | Menu bar and pull-downs |

### Use toolbars to supplement menus

Some toolbar items are used in conjunction with menu bars when users need a shortcut for certain actions. In these cases the toolbar items also appear on the menu bar.

### Use toolbars in place of some menu items

Some toolbar items can be used in place of menu items. For instance, some drawing tools cannot be described with words and would be difficult to place on a pull-down menu.

### Make toolbars consistent

If you use a toolbar throughout the application, or between applications, make sure you use the same button images for the same functions throughout.

### Make only active items available

Only toolbar items that are currently available should show. It is okay for some toolbar items to not show at all and for others to appear as users move from one part of the application to another. It is all right for some items on a toolbar to be grayed out if they are only temporarily unavailable.

### Allow users to move some toolbars

Allow users to move some toolbars to different locations on the screen to ensure they are out of the way of the work the users are doing.

### Allow users to toggle toolbars on and off

Let users turn toolbars on and off through a pull-down menu. This is especially important if you are providing more than one toolbar.

### Allow customizing

Consider allowing users to customize their toolbars by deciding what to put on or take off. You should, however, make decisions on what should be on the toolbar and provide that as the default. Most of the time, users should not have to customize a toolbar for it to be usable.

### *Use white space for grouping*

If some items on a toolbar go together, use white space to group them.

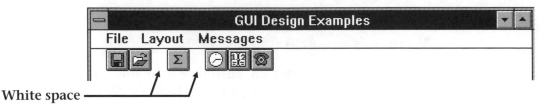

White space

### *Limit button images to 15*

A particular window should have 15 or fewer button images. Too many buttons create visual and cognitive strain. Users will just not see some if there are too many.

## List of Guidelines for Icons and Toolbars

### When to Use Icons

Use icons for a purpose

Use button images as shortcuts

Use icons when a picture is worth . . .

Use icons for international use

### Designing or Choosing Pictures

Decide on an approach

Develop a cohesive set

Include just enough detail for recognition

Use standard pictures

Consider changing the button image's state

Test your images

### Using Pictures in the Interface

Be consistent

Avoid words

Watch out for international meanings

### Toolbars

Use toolbars for frequent actions across screens

Use toolbars to supplement menus

Use toolbars in place of some menu items

Make toolbars consistent

Make only active items available

Allow users to move some toolbars

Allow users to toggle toolbars on and off

Allow customizing

Use white space for grouping

Limit button images to 15

# Metaphors

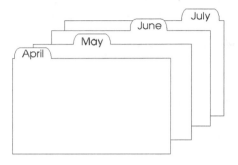

*Because graphical user interfaces allow the use of pictures and line drawings, it is easier to make metaphors obvious. Using the right metaphor can make dramatic differences in a GUI's usability. But what is the right metaphor? This chapter offers guidelines for making intelligent metaphor decisions.*

## Contents

## Use an Appropriate Metaphor

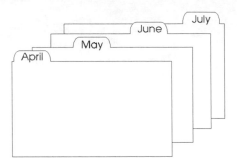

### Consider using metaphors

A metaphor is a visual representation, in your interface, of real-life objects. Metaphors do not act exactly like real objects. For example, the desktop metaphor is not exactly like a real desktop.

Using metaphors in GUIs can make the interface easier to use.

### Use industry-standard metaphors if they fit

There are a number of metaphors frequently used in graphical user interfaces that you may be able to extend. Some examples are:

- ❑ Desktop
- ❑ Spreadsheet
- ❑ Notebook
- ❑ Index cards
- ❑ Form (For example, an invoice form or a telephone answering pad.)

### Only use a metaphor within the users' world

A metaphor is useful only if the users know the real object that the metaphor is based on. Metaphors improve usability if they allow users to associate something unfamiliar (your application) with something they already know. The metaphor must be within the users' experience.

### *Choose metaphors carefully*

Talk to users to uncover the natural metaphors they already use:

- ☐ Ask them about the tasks they do and pay attention to the words they use.
- ☐ Listen for concrete objects they refer to.
- ☐ Listen for operations or actions they use.
- ☐ Listen for relationships between the objects and the actions.

### *Make sure metaphors work together*

It is all right to use more than one metaphor within an application. For instance, you could use a desktop, a folder, and a document together.

If you use more than one metaphor, however, make sure they all fit together into a meta-metaphor; for example, documents within folders.

### *Choose a metaphor that fits the task*

Make sure the metaphor you use fits the task. For example, do not use a baseball metaphor in an accounting application.

### *Use the metaphor consistently*

If you use a metaphor, maintain it consistently throughout the application. Use icons and graphics consistently to reinforce the metaphor.

### Don't rely on pictures alone

A metaphor is *not* the same as an icon. Although you may use visual elements to help communicate the metaphor, you do not have to. For example, an invoice form on a screen is a metaphor even if you can't make it look exactly like the actual form.

### Extend the metaphor if you need to

It is all right to extend a metaphor, that is, to go beyond the constraints of the actual physical object the metaphor represents. For example, folders in your interface could contain many things, not just documents.

### Explain the metaphors

Use documentation and training to explain and show examples of the metaphors.

### Test your metaphors

Make sure you test your metaphors with users. *Check your metaphor ideas early and often.*

### Avoid being unique

Metaphors work because they are simple. You do not have to come up with a new and unique idea, for example, that your database is just like a forest. Keep it simple and reuse ideas that work, like forms, spreadsheets, notebooks, and desktops.

## List of Guidelines for Metaphors

### Use an Appropriate Metaphor

Consider using metaphors
Use industry-standard metaphors if they fit
Only use a metaphor within the users' world
Choose metaphors carefully
Make sure metaphors work together
Choose a metaphor that fits the task
Use the metaphor consistently
Don't rely on pictures alone
Extend the metaphor if you need to
Explain the metaphors
Test your metaphors
Avoid being unique

# Chapter 9

# Fonts

Fonts
*Fonts*
FONTS

*With graphical user interfaces you have more choices in how to display text. This chapter summarizes good font decisions.*

## Contents

## Using Fonts Effectively

### Use a sans serif font

Use a sans serif font for text and labels. Sans serif is easier to read on screen.

**Serif:**

Times New Roman is a serif font. It has little feet on the letters.

**Sans serif:**

Arial is a sans serif font. It does not have little feet on the letters.

### Do not use italics or underlining

Italics and underlining can make text hard to read on a screen.

### Avoid using colored fonts

The easiest type to read is black type on a white background. If you mix colors of fonts on one screen, the colored type will be harder to read than the black. If you do use a colored font for a special purpose, consider bolding it to make it easier to read. See Chapter 6, *Color*, for more information.

### Use bold for emphasis

Use bolding of the body text for emphasis. Do not use color for emphasis because clients usually assume color is a cue for text with a different or specific purpose, such as a label or a hypertext link.

### Avoid changing font size

Avoid using font size to get attention. Many different fonts on one screen can be distracting.

### Use 10- and 12-point fonts

Use at least a 10-point font on screens. Many people have a hard time seeing fonts less than 10 points.

**Examples of point sizes:**

14 point

12 point

10 point

9 point

8 point

6 point

An exception is labels for icons. Labels for icons (including button images) can be a 9-point font.

### Minimize the number of different fonts

Limit the number of font types (typefaces). Try to use one font type for all text; using too many font types is confusing. For example, use all Arial, MS San Serif, or System.

# List of Guidelines for Fonts

## Using Fonts Effectively

Use a sans serif font

Do not use italics or underlining

Avoid using colored fonts

Use bold for emphasis

Avoid changing font size

Use 10- and 12-point fonts

Minimize the number of different fonts

# Chapter 05

# Visual Coding

| Detail Number |
|---|
| 00197617501 |
| 00248188800 |
| **00326696900** |
| 00997607001 |
| 01197654001 |
| 01597803501 |
| **01797659001** |

*Using highlighting to communicate information is called visual coding  Graphical user interfaces allow you to highlight and display information visually. This is a powerful advantage of GUIs that is often overlooked.*

## Contents

## Using Visual Coding Effectively

### Use visual coding for meaning

Use different types of highlighting and visual coding, for example, graying out, boldface, and reverse video, to convey specific meaning.

### Use graying out for unavailability

When controls, menu items, or button names are grayed out, then they are temporarily not available for the user to choose. Use graying out only to show temporary unavailability. If the item will never be available, then it should not appear at all.

Employer: [　　　　　　] ◀── Available

Employer: [　　　　　　] ◀────Temporarily protected and unavailable

### Use graying out for items that do not need attention

You can use graying out as a technique to show that an item in a list does not need attention. For example, to show a status that indicates the user does not have to make any changes.

### Use reverse video for high attention

Use reverse video for items that need immediate attention.

| Name | Location | Credit Number |
|------|----------|---------------|
| Berger's | 630 S. Church | 10056478 |
| Berger's | 415 Alexander | 10054777 |
| Bosco | 1 Bosco Way | 49596959 |
| Bosco | 16 Northern | 46650932 |

Reverse video ──▶

## *Use bold for items that need attention*

Use bold or dark text and graphics to imply that users should work on a particular item.

| Detail Analysis | | | | |
|---|---|---|---|---|

Customer ID: 13

Name:     Berger's Department Stores

| Detail Number | Name | Address | Credit Data | Bill Total |
|---|---|---|---|---|
| 00197617501 | Berger's Dept | 630 S. Church | 0000010008342 | $2,843.23 |
| 00248188800 | Berger's Dept | 1953 Wisconsin | 0000040005761 | $971.64 |
| **00326696900** | **Berger's Corp** | **29 S. Chicago** | **0000010009923** | **$15.91** |
| 00997607001 | Berger's Dept | 800 W. North | 0000010000115 | $2,248.33 |
| 01197654001 | Berger's Corp | 1005 Valley | 0000040006912 | $2,820.52 |
| 01597803501 | Berger's Corp | 1400 S. Main | 0000010004226 | $4,061.79 |
| **01797659001** | **Berger's Dept** | **630 S. Church** | **0000010002267** | **$4,009.05** |

## *Use boxes or borders to group or get attention*

Use boxes and borders to group items or to direct attention to critical items or messages.

## *Use all caps only for emphasis*

Sentences in all capital letters are 20 percent more difficult to read than sentences with upper- and lower-case letters. Avoid using all caps for large blocks of text. All caps can be effective, however, as a way of getting attention.

| | |
|---|---|
| **Do this** | This is an example of text in mixed case. It is easier to read than all caps. |
| **Don't do this** | THIS IS AN EXAMPLE OF TEXT IN ALL CAPS. IT IS HARDER TO READ THAN MIXED CASE. |
| **Use for warnings** | DO NOT REMOVE |

### *Avoid blinking*

Blinking on a screen is very powerful as an attention getter and also very annoying. Only use blinking if:

❏ You need to get the user's attention immediately before a serious and destructive action occurs.

❏ Users can turn it off easily.

❏ You only blink in one location at a time.

## List of Guidelines for Visual Coding

### Using Visual Coding Effectively

Use visual coding for meaning

Use graying out for unavailability

Use graying out for items that do not need attention

Use reverse video for high attention

Use bold for items that need attention

Use boxes or borders to group or get attention

Use all caps only for emphasis

Avoid blinking

# Chapter 1

# *Graphing*

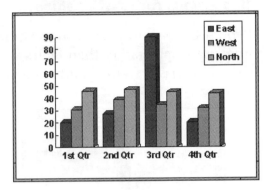

*Graphical user interfaces allow you to show data visually using charts and graphs. This chapter demonstrates how to use charts and graphs effectively.*

## Contents

# When to Use Graphs

## Use graphs for relationships

If you need to show relationships among different categories or over time, use graphs rather than tables with specific values. People can grasp trends faster from a graph than from interpreting data in a table.

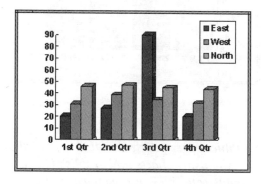

## Use tables for specific values

If users need to find a particular value, use a table rather than a graph.

|        | 1st Qtr | 2nd Qtr | 3rd Qtr | 4th Qtr |
|--------|---------|---------|---------|---------|
| East   | 20.4    | 27.4    | 90      | 20.4    |
| West   | 30.6    | 38.6    | 34.6    | 31.6    |
| North  | 45.9    | 46.9    | 45      | 43.9    |

# Designing a Graph

## Use bar graphs for categories

If you have discrete categories and are trying to show the relationship between them, use a bar graph.

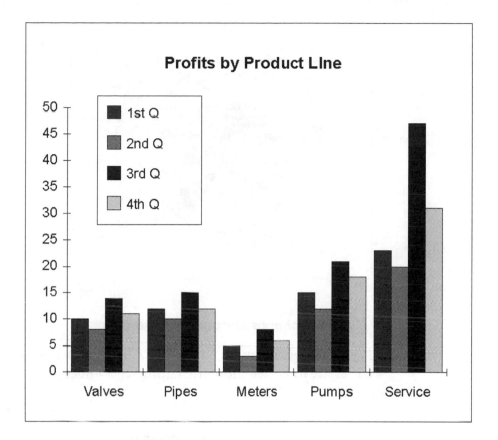

Bar graphs can also show multiple relationships between categories.

## Use special effects carefully

Use 3-D effects only if they help communicate the information. Avoid fancy formats if they don't help the user understand the data.

## Use a pie chart for part-to-whole relationships

If you want to show part-to-whole relationships, use a pie chart.

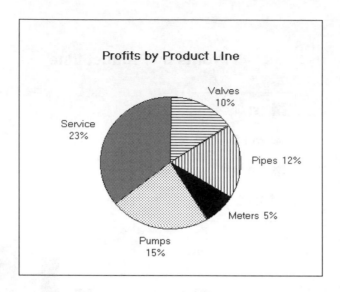

## Use line charts for continuous data

If you have continuous data, use a line chart rather than a pie or bar chart to better show the cumulative effect.

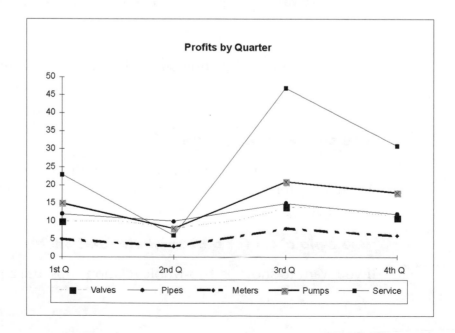

### Choose appropriate scales

Choose an appropriate scale for both the X and Y axes of graphs. If the scale is too expanded, you may be exaggerating the effect. If the scale is too small, you may be underreporting the effect.

### Consider displaying specific values

If users need to see a specific value as well as a general trend or relationship, show the exact values on the graph itself.

### Use visual coding on graphs

Use color, highlighting, shading, or patterns to distinguish parts of a graph.

### Use legends for complicated graphs

If graphs have a lot of data and a lot of visual coding, use a legend.

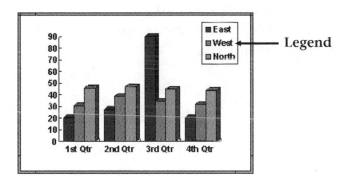

### Label graphs and data

Label the graph with terminology users will understand. Consider the following labels:

❑ Graph title

❑ Lines, bars, or parts of the pie

❑ X axis

❑ Y axis

# List of Guidelines for Graphing

### When to Use Graphs

Use graphs for relationships

Use tables for specific values

### Designing a Graph

Use bar graphs for categories

Use special effects carefully

Use a pie chart for part-to-whole relationships

Use line charts for continuous data

Choose appropriate scales

Consider displaying specific values

Use visual coding on graphs

Use legends for complicated graphs

Label graphs and data

# Chapter 12

# Navigation and Interaction

When you design an interface, you require users to move through and interact with applications in a certain way and in a certain order. How well you design that process determines to a large extent how easy the interface is to use. This chapter describes critical guidelines for navigation and interaction.

## Contents

Making Navigation Decisions

Pointing Devices and Keyboard Support

List of Guidelines for Navigation and Interaction

## Making Navigation Decisions

 ### *Match the users' work flow*

Make sure that the order of windows, menus, screens, and dialog boxes fits the way the users do their work. Do not make the users change the way they work to fit your interface.

 ### *Choose and show an obvious path*

Even though you want to build in flexibility, it is critical that you pick a *best path* through the application and make that path obvious. This best path should be based on what most users want to do most of the time. You can then use options, choices, and alternatives to provide flexibility for the rest of the tasks.

Too much flexibility results in confused users.

### *Use an appropriate unit of work*

People like to start and finish a task in one session. Think about each series of dialog boxes and windows as representing one unit of work. Don't break up the dialog boxes into pieces that are too small, but also do not tackle too large a unit of work in one place.

 ### *Find a home*

The home is the screen or window users come back to again and again while working on a particular task.

Decide on a window that will serve as the users' home. The home might be a screen of data, a list, or a form with or without data. Home is not necessarily the first window they see when they enter the application or a particular task. Users might go through a series of selection and list screens before reaching home.

Do not make home a blank screen with a menu bar. It should be a screen with meaningful information for the task they are performing, such as a list of contracts or a blank invoice form.

Having a home helps users remember what to do, gives them a concrete and visual anchor point, and helps alleviate the feeling of being lost in the interface.

## Pointing Devices and Keyboard Support

### Provide support for both pointing and keyboards

Provide support for both pointing devices and keyboards by providing both keyboard equivalents and accelerators.

### Design for one device

Even though you are providing both pointing and keyboard support, design each part of the application to best fit one or the other. At any given part of the application you should decide whether most users are going to be typing or pointing. Then make your other decisions (grouping, choice of controls, layout) based on that decision.

It is all right to have the focus change as someone moves through the application (for example, primarily use the keyboard on one set of windows and a mouse on another), but avoid having users go back and forth continually in one window or set of windows to perform a unit of work.

### Consider right-mouse clicks

Right-mouse clicking is becoming a common addition to the user interface. For instance, pointing at a screen object and pressing the right-mouse button can invoke a pop-up menu.

You may want to allow the user to customize the right-mouse button as a shortcut to common actions like opening a frequently used dialog box.

## List of Guidelines for Navigation and Interaction

### Making Navigation Decisions

Match the users' work flow

Choose and show an obvious path

Use an appropriate unit of work

Find a home

### Pointing Devices and Keyboard Support

Provide support for both pointing and keyboard

Design for one device

Consider right-mouse clicks

# *Online Help*

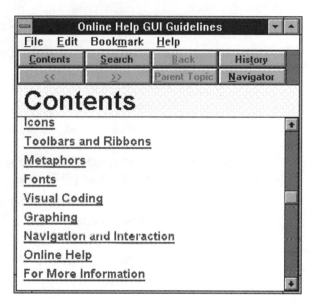

*There are many types of online information: reference manuals, tutorials, context-sensitive help, and hypertext help systems. These guidelines apply to standard help systems.*

## Contents

# What to Put Online

## *Use help for the right kind of information*

There are many types of online information—entire reference manuals, tutorials, context-sensitive help, and hypertext help systems.

### Help

Online help systems are designed to support applications although they can be used for other purposes, such as company procedures. The cue cards present in some new software packages support users as they work through complex tasks. These are an example of help files, as is context-sensitive help. Users go to these systems for information on how to perform specific tasks and actions. These are the systems these guidelines support.

### Document viewers

Another way of delivering information online is document-viewing systems. This method is appropriate for large amounts of information, presented in a format just like the document's printed pages, which needs to be viewed and printed from a variety of platforms. This method solves many distribution problems but is not appropriate as an online help system. These guidelines do not apply to document-viewing systems.

### Multimedia

Multimedia, an excellent tool for training, is also not addressed in these guidelines. Multimedia approaches can be added to Windows help systems through the use of OLE (Object Linking and Embedding) but the standards for their development are not included in these guidelines.

### Know your platform

Windows and OS/2 help systems, while accomplishing the same purpose, do it quite differently. Study existing help systems in your platform so that you understand clearly the capabilities and limitations your platform imposes on you as a help author.

There are many software tools available for Windows to help assist you in the tedious formatting of topics for online viewing. There are not many of these tools for OS/2.

### Consider users' needs

People go to online help for quick and current answers to immediate problems. However, current research has shown that for most people, reading online is slower and harder than reading from paper.

Consider the following points when deciding what types of information to put online.

### Put online

- ❏ Urgent information
- ❏ Specific information
- ❏ Information that changes frequently
- ❏ Complexly organized information
- ❏ Large amounts of reference information
- ❏ Documentation for the physically challenged

### Don't put online

- ❏ Large amounts of conceptual information
- ❏ Getting started information

❑ Information requiring lengthy or detailed reading

❑ Information needed off line

# Writing for Online

### *Use documentation professionals*

Consider using documentation professionals to write your online help. They are trained to keep the perspectives and needs of your users as their highest priority. They are skilled at presenting information designed for usability.

### *Decide how much paper you will provide*

Decide up front if your users need the information on paper or not. Your options are:

❑ Provide the same content on paper and online.

❑ Provide extensive online information and minimal paper.

❑ Limit paper to what users choose to print.

Creating online help and paper documentation from the same source file is possible, and helps with version control if this is your goal. However, you will have to make some tradeoffs between efficiency and the best possible product for each medium.

### *Diagram the entire help system before writing*

Sketch a diagram of the help system before you begin writing. Create the main contents screen, and then show all the jumps. Continue through the help system showing how many clicks the users have to make to get to the information they need.

### *Limit the number of heading levels*

Limit the number of heading levels and the amount of indentation. If you use too many indentations, you will require the user to use too many clicks to get to required information.

### *Keep text concise*

Make it easy for your readers by eliminating all unnecessary words and detail. It is harder to read online than on paper for the following reasons.

❑ A screen, especially a help panel, displays less information than a paper page.

❑ Text resolution online is less clear than on paper.

❑ Glare from monitors causes eye strain, especially if users are trying to read a lot of text.

❑ Far-sighted people may have to tip their heads to read online, causing neck strain if they must do it for too long.

### *Keep topics short*

Try not to make the users scroll to read the entire topic. Try to limit a topic to one help panel. Remember that your screen real estate is limited.

### *Create standalone chunks*

A piece of information presented online must be able to stand alone.

❑ Write each topic so that it does not depend on a previous chunk of information for its meaning.

❑ Use one main idea for each topic.

❑ Create links to related information.

### Design for access

- ❏ Hierarchical structure gives users clear mental models and helps you organize your information. A table of contents is one example of hierarchical information.
- ❏ Linking (like paper cross references) allows users to move from topic to topic, following their own path to the information they need.
- ❏ Keyword search (index) allows users to go directly to specific information, just like an index in a book.

### Organize information for quick access and comprehension

Users must be able to find information within seconds. If they cannot find what they need quickly, they will stop using the online help.

- ❏ Design the system so that no more than three clicks are required to get to any information.
- ❏ Provide multiple paths to the same information. Write a chunk of information once but build many routes to that chunk.
- ❏ Write concisely so that the information can be read quickly.
- ❏ Index thoroughly.

### Be consistent

Consistency in the organization and presentation of information is important in all professional writing, but is especially important when writing for online use.

Be consistent in all your user cues. For example, always use boldface and colors to cue the reader to the same information, and always construct similar topics with the same information in the same order.

### Use active voice

Active voice creates stronger and shorter sentences than does passive voice.

| | |
|---|---|
| **Change this** | When the Search button is clicked, topics are displayed. |
| **To this** | Click Search. From the Search dialog box, select your topic. |

### Use present tense

Present tense is more direct and more powerful than past, future, or conditional tenses.

| | |
|---|---|
| **Change this** | When you click the Search button the topics will appear. |
| **To this** | Click Search. The topics appear. |

### Use the informal pronoun you

Address the reader directly. The second person pronoun creates a friendlier tone and it helps you avoid using gender-specific pronouns. It also helps you avoid writing in the passive voice.

| | |
|---|---|
| **Change this** | The user has a number of actions he can take at this point. |
| **To this** | Now you can take a number of actions. |

### Write effective procedures

If you are putting procedures online, be sure they include the same elements that create good paper procedures. Effective online procedures contain the following information:

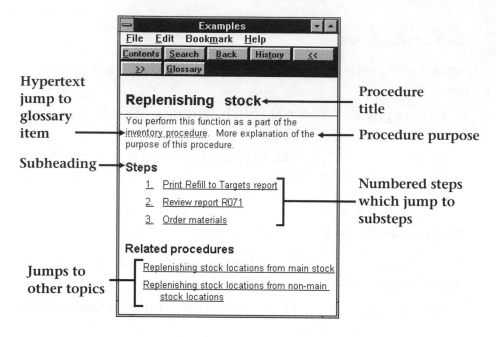

Hypertext jump to glossary item

Subheading

Jumps to other topics

Procedure title

Procedure purpose

Numbered steps which jump to substeps

Procedures may also include any of the following:

- ❑ Frequency of procedure
- ❑ Title of person responsible for procedure
- ❑ Required preceding tasks or other background information necessary to perform the task
- ❑ Information on how this procedure affects other system functions
- ❑ If this is an online procedure, the menu choices that bring the user to the correct screens

## How to make a help file

### Design

1. Design the entire online help system with an outline and quick paper sketches.
2. Create a prototype of a small portion of the real information. Test the prototype.

### Develop

3. Write and format the text in a word processor.

4. Add graphics.

5. Code the file using a help tool to automate many of the coding functions.

6. Compile the file.

7. Review and revise.

8. Recompile.

### Test and distribute

9. Test and revise.

10. Prepare final files and distribute.

## Windows and Pop-ups

Windows and OS/2 provide different approaches to help systems. In Windows you, as the help author, can use a number of different window styles for different types of information: main windows, secondary windows, and pop-ups.

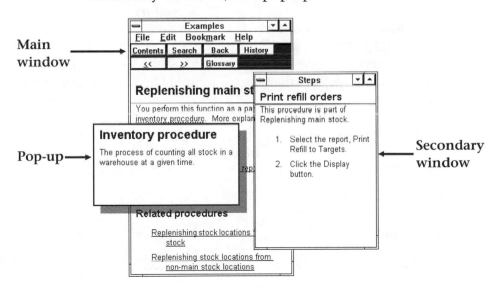

In OS/2 there are index windows and topics windows. Glossary items appear in a topic window rather than in a pop-up as they do in Windows help systems.

Initial contents window ——

Search results contents ——

Topic ——

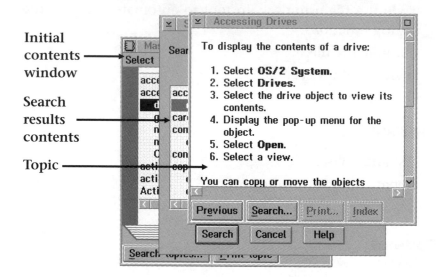

## Understand how each Windows display type works

| Function | Main window | Secondary window | Pop-up |
|---|---|---|---|
| Display style | Remains open all the time | Remains open until closed | Displays over window containing hot spot |
| Number of shape and placement definitions | One definition; user can modify | Up to five definitions; user can modify | One definition |
| Access methods | | | |
| Hotspots in text | Yes | Yes | Yes |
| Keyword search | Yes | You decide | No |
| Topic lists | Yes | You decide | Yes |

| Function | Main window | Secondary window | Pop-up |
|---|---|---|---|
| Size | You define; user can modify | You define; user can modify | Automatically sizes to fit text, limited to length of one screen |
| Scrolls | Yes | Yes | No |
| Position | You define; user can modify | You define; user can modify | Below hotspot |
| Colors | You define | You define | None |
| Caption | Help file title | You define | None |
| Menu bar | Yes | No | No |
| Button bar | Yes | You can create | No |
| Title | Yes | Yes | Yes |
| Nonscrolling region possible | Yes | Yes | No |
| How to close | Closing window closes Help | Windows close commands | Click anywhere |
| How to print | From File menu | You must code the print function | Can't |

Note: As the help tools evolve, their functionality will expand.

## Use different Windows display types for specific information

- ❏ Determine the type of information you will display in each type of the above windows or pop-ups.
- ❏ Define different secondary windows for different purposes.
- ❏ Consider using colors in nonscrolling areas to distinguish between main and secondary windows.

Decide whether users will want to print secondary windows. If they are to print, you may need to code a button or icon.

## Main Contents Window

In Windows the first thing users see after they click Help on the menu bar of their application is a main contents window. You can design this window to show whatever topics you want and can also add graphics. It lists the name of the help file, has its own menu bar and buttons, and lists high-level contents items. Each contents item is a jump to that topic's information.

First window
in Windows
help file

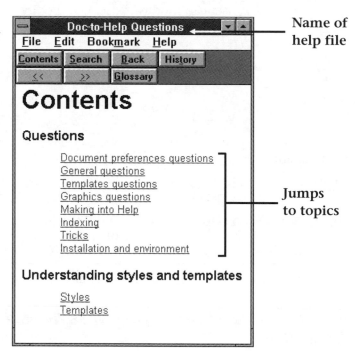

Name of
help file

Jumps
to topics

In OS/2 the first thing users see is an index list. Because you cannot modify this list, the guidelines in this topic apply only to the Windows environment.

**First window in OS/2 help file**

## Include the following types of topic titles

In a large help system in Windows you will need to carefully plan the items to appear on the main contents window. You want to get the users to the right information quickly, with no more than three clicks, but having to read through too many items will slow them down.

Try to include the following on the main contents window:

❑ Content used frequently by most users

❑ Critical information

❑ Information specific to a group of users

❑ Substeps only if there is room without scrolling

## Design the main contents window

Design with usability in mind. Users want to make quick but accurate choices.

❑ Include only the topic titles that will fit on one panel. Try to avoid making users scroll.

❑ Group contents items if there are more than seven of them.

❑ Label each group. Limit topics to fewer than eight in any one group.

❑ Try to avoid putting more than fifteen topics on the contents screen.

❑ Separate items and groups with enough white space to make them easy for users to read.

❑ Word each content item clearly so that users will immediately know what that topic contains and will not pick a wrong topic.

See the *Conventions* and *Color* sections of this chapter for guidelines on color and fonts.

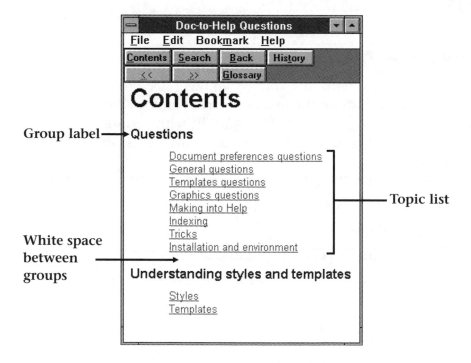

### Consider using graphics

Graphics used with words can increase the help system's usability. Beginning users read the words. Experienced users access the topics via the graphics, because the brain processes graphics faster than words. See Chapter 7, *Icons and Toolbars*, for more information on designing graphics.

❑ Select graphics that truly represent the topic.

❑ Be careful not to offend any individual or group. Be especially careful if your product has an international audience.

❑ Keep the graphics simple.

### Use pull-down menus

Pull-down menus allow users access to features used less frequently than those on the button bar, such as user annotation and book-mark placement. They also:

❑ Group related functions.

❑ Economize on screen space.

❑ Indicate the status of toggle functions.

### Provide a unique mnemonic

Use the first letter of the menu name or an internal consonant as a keyboard equivalent. Place an underline under the mnemonic.

## Button Bar

### Use the button bar for continual access to actions or topics

Since in Windows the button bar appears on every main window, you can use buttons to allow users access to information from anywhere in the help system. You can add buttons to or delete buttons from the button bar, depending on the needs of your users.

Secondary windows do not have buttons unless you create them.

**Button bar in Windows help**

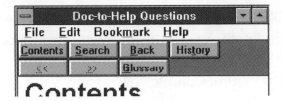

OS/2 does not use a button bar, but does have buttons that appear at the bottom of its windows. In its topic window there are buttons for navigating and printing.

**Buttons in OS/2 help**

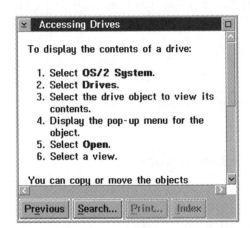

## Use standard Windows buttons

Buttons found in most Windows help systems include:

| Button | Purpose |
|--------|---------|
| Contents | Returns users to the main contents screen or other screen you define |
| Search | Access the keyword search (index) feature |

| Button | Purpose |
| --- | --- |
| Back | Steps users back in order through main windows that have displayed |
| History | Allows users to see all the help windows they have chosen and select one from the list |
| << and >> (Browse) | Moves users backward and forward through a browse sequence. This is usually the linear order of the information. |
| Glossary | Lists terms you have defined as glossary items |

### Create new buttons

If your Windows system needs additional functionality on the button bar you can create new buttons. For instance, you may want a button for field definitions that contains a list separate from your glossary.

# Links

### Link your application to help

Linking an application directly to help is called *context-sensitive* help. Users press a key, such as F1, to get help on a field or object in the application. After accessing help from the application users can move to any part of the help file.

### Link topics together

Link topics to each other in two basic ways.

❑ Code a word, phrase, or graphic as a hotspot and link it to another topic. When users click on the hotspot they jump to the linked topic.

❏ In Windows you can list additional topics below your text and code them as hotspots. When users click on the title, they jump to that topic.

### Create pop-ups for terms in the topics

In Windows help you can use pop-ups—small windows that come up over part of the window you are using and are then dismissed by the next keystroke or click.

One use of pop-ups is for defining terms and fields.

### Use graphics as hotspots

In Windows you can make an entire graphic a hotspot, or you can make portions of a graphic individual hotspots that jump to different topics or pop-ups.

For example, you could show a toolbar from your application and make each icon on the toolbar a hotspot that jumps to a discussion of that icon. Another example is a flow chart in which each box is a hotspot jumping to the topic for that box.

### Plan your index carefully

Windows and OS/2 use a keyword search function to allow users to jump to the exact information they need. *Keywords* are words you, as the help author, identify, much like you create index terms. See the section in this chapter on *Keyword Search*.

❏ Think carefully about how users will want to search for information.

❏ Some help tools automatically include the topic title in the keyword search list. Know how your tool works and how you can control this feature. Consider this when indexing terms in a topic.

### Link files to other files within a help system

A Windows help file can be composed of multiple files created individually, then combined in the final compile process. You can use all the forms of jumps to move the user from topic to topic across files.

### Connect one help system to another help system

In Windows you can build limited links between separate help project files. You can create buttons to allow the users to jump from one file to another, but you cannot link topics or glossary terms directly.

### Link help systems to external programs

You can launch another program from within a help file. Use this for multimedia tutorials or application demonstrations.

### Limit the number of hotspots

Too many hotspots (text marked as a hypertext link) can make it hard to read the topic. They can also distract the reader from the immediate topic by suggesting too many side trips.

## Context-Sensitive Help

### Use map numbers to link the application to the help file

When you create a help file each topic receives a context string, which is simply a label identifying this topic. Application developers enter this identifying number into their code, thereby linking a specific screen element to the correct help topic.

Some help tools have a drag-and-drop feature for creating map numbers in both the application and the help file.

### You can use several help files

You can link several different context-sensitive help files to the same application, but make sure all the context IDs are unique.

## Glossaries

The traditional glossary is a list of terms and their definitions. This can include business terms, field definitions, screen descriptions, or any other list of items you need to define. Definitions are customarily displayed as pop-ups, but can also be displayed as topics in windows.

Glossary
hotspot and
pop-up in
Windows

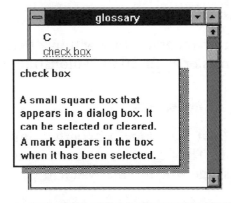

Glossary
hotspot
selected, in
OS/2

Glossary
item in OS/2

## Multiple glossaries

You can have multiple glossaries by making each its own file and placing a button for each glossary on the button bar. For instance, you might have one glossary for business terms and another for field descriptions.

## Use alphabetical buttons

If your glossary is large, you may want to help users by creating buttons to take them quickly to a specific group of definitions. The most common use of this method is alphabetical buttons.

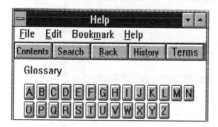

## Avoid coding a glossary term too often

Some help tools code every occurrence of a word as a glossary item. This may cause the word to appear as a hotspot repeatedly in the same topic. If this happens, find a way to trick the tool. For instance, add an extra letter at the end of the occurrences of the word that you don't want made into hotspots and then make that letter hidden text. Then, the help tool will not tag these words as hotspots.

## Keyword Search

### *Allow enough time*

Most users rely on the keyword search function (index) of online help to find information quickly. Because of this it is important that you allocate a large amount of your development effort to indexing, about 10 percent of the total.

### *How it works*

In Windows, when users select a term from the keyword list, all the topic titles that include that index reference are listed in the second list box. It is important that index terms be clear and consistent and that topic titles be descriptive.

Windows help search dialog box

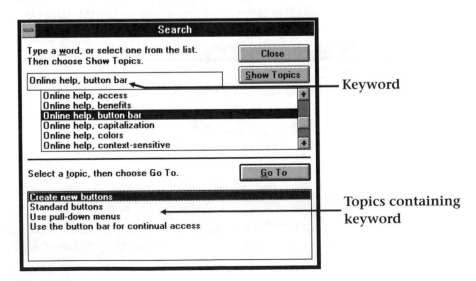

Keyword

Topics containing keyword

In OS/2 the interface is somewhat different when searching from a topic window or an index list. Clicking on the Search button from a topic window causes the following dialog box to display.

OS/2 help search dialog box

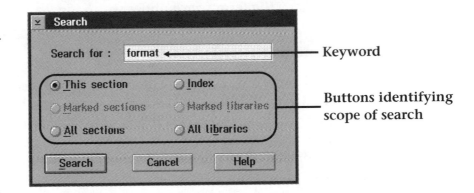

Selecting an item from the index list causes a list of topics for that item to display, as shown below.

OS/2 help search list

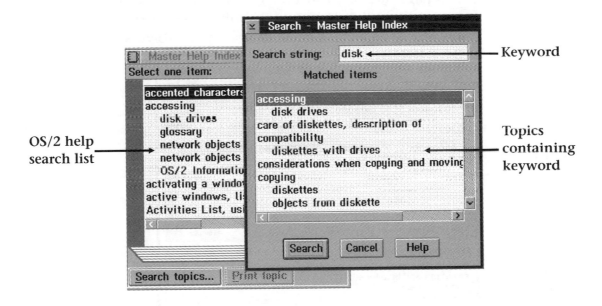

## Think like your users

Imagine how users will want to look up information. Do not assume they are coming from the same knowledge base that you are. For instance, index the term *search* under *search, find,* and *look up.*

## Be selective in your indexing

Do not include every occurrence of a word. Using a *concordance* (a list of terms to be indexed) creates a poor index. You need to index only important occurrences of a term.

However, you want to be sure that you provide enough keywords. A general guide is three to four times the number of information topics.

## Nest index terms

Just as in paper it is not useful to a user to look something up and see 10 page numbers listed after a term, it does not help a user to see many topics listed for a term in online help. Nesting index terms helps the user select the exact subject matter to view.

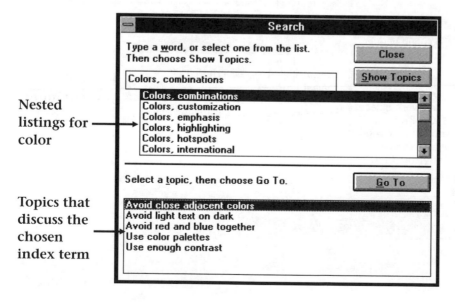

If a single keyword returns more than seven topics, the reader must scroll to see them all. Subdividing, or nesting, the keywords minimizes this problem.

## Use synonyms

Identify words that are synonyms for the word you are indexing and include them in the list.

## Maintain a list of words you are indexing

Create a list of the terms you are indexing and use this to maintain consistency in terms, verbs, plurals, and capitalization.

### Verb forms

Decide whether to create keywords from the second person form of verbs (*Open files*) or from the gerund (*Opening files*). Most help authors use gerunds.

### Plurals

Decide whether you will use the singular (*File*) or plural (*Files*) form of nouns.

### Capitalization

Decide whether to capitalize the keywords or not. In paper indexes it is common to capitalize the highest level of the term but not the nested term.

## Understand your tool

Have a thorough understanding of how your help tool creates the keyword search list.

## Control topic titles

Most help tools automatically add topic titles to the keyword search. Check to see if your tool allows you to control this function.

If you use the topic title as a keyword, you may need to rephrase the title so that the most important word appears first. You may also want to offer the title a second way, inverted. For instance, you might list it as *Saving files* and as *Files, saving*.

### Test your index

Perform a usability test on your index, preferably with real users. Observe them trying to look up topics. They will try to look up topics under terms that match their work and thought processes. This information will help you improve the keyword search function.

# Navigation

### Don't let users get lost

It is easy for users to get lost in help systems. As they jump from hypertext link to hypertext link they may lose track of where they are. Poorly written topics may not stand alone, making it hard for users to know how a topic fits into the total system.

Some recent tools for Windows help have included an outline feature that users can invoke. This feature allows them to see where any given topic fits into the total set of information.

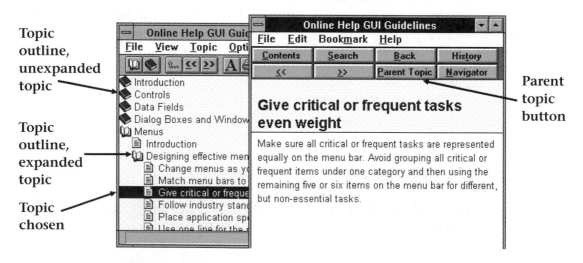

Topic outline, unexpanded topic

Topic outline, expanded topic

Topic chosen

Parent topic button

### Allow users to move up the hierarchy

Another way to help users navigate without getting lost is to give them a button that takes them to the contents list for a set of topics rather than the main contents for the entire help system.

Another similar use of buttons is one that allows users to go to the parent topic for the topic they are viewing. In the example in the previous guideline, clicking on the Parent Topic button would take the user to Designing Effective Menus.

## Screen Images and Graphics

### Use images of screens judiciously

You may want to put images of application icons, button images, dialog boxes, and even whole screens into your online help. Do it cautiously.

- ❑ Screen and button images in online help can confuse users. They may look like the real thing, and users may try to click on them.
- ❑ This can be one of the more time consuming parts of your effort.

### Use a screen-grab program

Use a screen-grab program to take pictures of your application screens and button images for use in the online help. Some help tools come with screen grabbers and there are many packages on the market that do this.

Use one that will allow you to grab small sections of the screen and look for a tool that will allow you to grab a pull-down menu. Screen grabbers with these capabilities exist in some of the online help tools for Windows.

### Use monochrome images

Unless you really need color, place monochrome images in help. This will help lessen user confusion. Set your Windows display to monochrome or alter the images in a paint program.

### Clean up your images

Use a paint program to trim the image and repaint or delete parts of the image.

### Do not scale bitmapped images

Use a .WMF file or import the .BMP image into a drawing package and scale it there. Bitmaps that have been made larger or smaller do not display clearly onscreen, although they will print clearly.

### Place bitmaps by reference

If you use an image more than once, store the image outside the text file and refer to the same stored image each time.

### Answer these questions before adding graphics

Before adding graphics to your help file, consider the needs of your readers and your purpose.  Justify, from a usability perspective, every graphic in your file.

- ❏ What is the purpose of this graphic? How will it help the user?
- ❏ Will the graphics be color or monochrome?
- ❏ How will you capture or create the graphics? What software will you use? (The files must be either .BMP or .WMF.)
- ❏ Will you need to resize the images?
- ❏ How easily does your help tool handle graphics?

❑ Will you be using the images as hotspots? The whole image or segments of it? How does your tool handle this?

❑ Is your file size an issue? Graphics will significantly increase the size of your help files.

## Color

### *Use color for substantive reasons only*

Do not use color just to make things look pretty. Color should be used to cue users about specific information. Use it to:

❑ Help users identify specific types of information, such as jump hotspots.

❑ Call attention to important information, such as warnings.

### *Consider these problems*

Use colors carefully, remembering the problems as well as the benefits.

❑ How colors display depends on the users' Windows environment settings.

❑ Some users are partially or completely color blind.

❑ Colors can distract from the text and make it harder to read.

### *Use no more than three colors*

Minimize the number of cues that users must remember. Users will be trying to learn information from your help system and should not be bothered by having to struggle to remember what your cues mean.

### Do not use color alone to cue readers

To avoid problems with color blindness and varying color displays, accompany color with other character formatting, such as underlining.

### Use color consistently

Use color consistently across all parts of your help system.

### Use familiar color codes

Consider the culture of your audience. Use color associations that are common and not offensive to a particular culture. For instance, in the United States, use red for warnings and cautions.

### Test your use of color

Test your colors by viewing them in monochrome display mode. Other tests include using color-blind subjects, and, to test the effectiveness of your color choices, use subjects familiar with other help systems.

### Follow industry standards to code hotspots

Code hotspots (hypertext jump text) in the manner common for your platform. Using colors that differ from the standard will impose another learning task on your users.

# Testing

## *Test the entire file thoroughly*

Test each of the following items before considering your help file complete. It is best to test early and often. If you save it until last, you may find you do not have time to correct serious errors.

Test the entire file. Keep a printed copy of your help file and write down problem areas as you find them. Make the corrections, recompile, and test again. And again.

- ❑ Test all the jumps between topics. Do the jumps go where they should? Do the links make sense?

- ❑ Read each topic after jumping to it. Does the topic make sense in isolation? Does the heading clearly indicate the contents?

- ❑ Check pop-ups. Do the words tagged as glossary items make sense? Are there too many tags? Make sure the glossary term is not tagged in its own definition.

- ❑ Check the length of glossary items. Does all the text fit in the pop-up box?

- ❑ Check the topic length. Are any topics too long? Can you break the topic into subtopics?

- ❑ Check your clicks. How many clicks does it take to get to a topic? Try to keep to three or fewer, if at all possible.

- ❑ Check formatting. Have you followed your standards? Is each kind of text formatted the way you want it?

- ❑ Check tables. Do they display easily, so that readers can see all the information without horizontal scrolling or changing the window size?

- ❑ Check graphics. Does the graphic fit in the window? Does the image have a clean appearance? Does the graphic look so much like the application image that it will confuse readers?

❑ Check graphic jumps. If you used parts of an image as hotspots, check each one.

❑ Test your keyword search terms. Did you select terms in a consistent manner? Are too many terms associated with just one topic? Are too many topics listed for a term? Does the topic listed for a term make sense?

## Conventions

### *Check recent commercial help systems*

Many conventions for online help will change as the technology evolves. Check recent help systems included with commercial software to try out new techniques. Assess the new techniques for their effectiveness before including them in your system.

### *Capitalization*

❑ Never use all caps, except for acronyms and initializations. Words in all caps are harder to read.

❑ Decide on capitalization patterns for words in topic titles and for the first words in lists. Be consistent.

❑ It is preferable to have keyword search terms begin with a capital letter.

### *Fonts for different text*

❑ Use Arial or MS Sans Serif.

    Arial

    MS Sans Serif

❑ Use a font size of 10 points for body text.

    Arial, 10 points

❑ Make titles 14 points, bold, no underline.

## Arial, 14 points, bold

### Type characteristics

❑ Use bolding for titles and to call attention to special words or phrases.

❑ Avoid using underlining for emphasis as it is used to indicate jumps and pop-ups.

### Tables

❑ Display large tables in a secondary window defined to be wide enough to display the width of the table. If your tool allows the table text to wrap within its cell you may not need to use a special secondary window.

❑ Help compilers often do not support lines. If you want borders with your tables, create the tables in a spreadsheet and then import the table as a picture.

### Unsupported characters

Help compilers often do not recognize:

| Unsupported character | Solution |
| --- | --- |
| Curly quotes or curly apostrophes | Use feet and inches key |
| Em and en dashes | Use hyphens |
| Superscript and subscript | Create a bitmap |
| Text typed with Caps Lock key on | Type with the Shift key |
| Fill justified text | Use left-justified text |
| Decimal or leader tabs | Don't use these |
| Borders and shading | Use bitmapped graphics |

## List of Guidelines for Online Help

### What to Put Online

Use help for the right kind of information
Know your platform
Consider user needs
Put online
Don't put online

### Writing for Online

Use documentation professionals
Decide how much paper you will provide
Diagram the entire help system before writing
Limit the number of heading levels
Keep text concise
Keep topics short
Create standalone chunks
Design for access
Organize information for quick access and comprehension
Be consistent
Use active voice
Use present tense
Use the informal pronoun *you*
Write effective procedures
How to make a help file

### Windows and Pop-ups

Understand how each Windows display type works
Use different Windows display types for specific information

### Main Contents Window

Include the following types of topic titles
Design the main contents window

Consider using graphics

Use pull-down menus

Provide a unique mnemonic

### Button Bar

Use the button bar for continual access to actions or topics

Use standard Windows buttons

Create new buttons

### Links

Link your application to help

Link topics together

Create pop-ups for terms in the topics

Use graphics as hotspots

Plan your index carefully

Link files to other files within a help system

Connect one help system to another help system

Link help systems to external programs

Limit the number of hotspots

### Context-Sensitive Help

Use map numbers to link the application to the help file

You can use several help files

### Glossaries

Multiple glossaries

Use alphabetical buttons

Avoid coding a glossary term too often

### Keyword Search

Allow enough time

How it works

Think like your users

Be selective in your indexing

Nest index terms

Use synonyms

Maintain a list of words you are indexing

Understand your tool

Control topic titles

Test your index

## Navigation

Don't let users get lost

Allow users to move up the hierarchy

## Screen Images and Graphics

Use images of screens judiciously

Use a screen-grab program

Use monochrome images

Clean up your images

Do not scale bitmapped images

Place bitmaps by reference

Answer these questions before adding graphics

## Color

Use color for substantive reasons only

Consider these problems

Use no more than three colors

Do not use color alone to cue readers

Use color consistently

Use familiar color codes

Test your use of color

Follow industry standards to code hotspots

## Testing

Test the entire file thoroughly

## Conventions

Check recent commercial help systems

Capitalization

Fonts for different text

Type characteristics

Tables

Unsupported characters

# Chapter 14

# *Customization Guide*

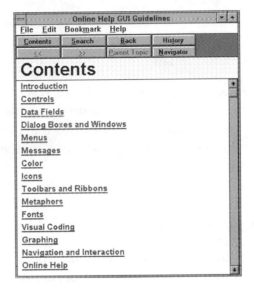

You can use this book as is to begin improving your GUI applications immediately. But for even more consistency across your enterprise, consider customizing these guidelines for your organization. You can purchase a license for this book that allows you to make text and picture changes to the disk files.

This chapter walks you through the process of customizing and implementing your own guidelines.

## Contents

**Getting Started**

**Starting the Process**

**Project Planning for Customizing Guidelines**

**Rolling Out and Implementing Guidelines**

## What to Customize

You can use this book as a template for your own enterprise-wide guidelines. Here are some of the changes and additions you may want to make:

### Button names

Consider adding to the list of reserved words for button names. Look at your existing systems or prototypes, talk to your developers and users, and decide on additional names you may want to add to the list. Decide on any button names you want to change or delete from the list.

### Adding menu-bar items

Consider choosing additional menu-bar items if you repeatedly have action categories that occur across a lot of applications.

### Decide on File versus a more specific name

Decide whether you want to require that applications use the word *File* rather than a more specific name on the menu bar.

### Tool restrictions

If your current GUI programming tools do not allow you to follow some of the guidelines in this book, you will need to decide whether you are going to:

- ❑ Take out that guideline.
- ❑ Leave it in with a note that your current environment cannot support.

### Pictures and screen captures

One of the most powerful ways that you can customize the guidelines is to include some of your own real or prototype screens in place of, or in addition to, the screens that are in this book. The more of your screens that you can provide, the better. This is not an all-or-none idea. You might use the screens provided in the files that accompany this book and add in additional ones of your own, or replace some of ours with some of yours.

### Icons and button images

You may want to include particular icons and button images.

### Adding in a contact name and phone number

The sections in this chapter on rolling out, implementing, maintaining, and updating guidelines suggest that you identify a person to act as contact for the guidelines. You may want to include this person's name and number in your book.

### Feedback form

You may want to include a form for users or developers to fill out and send in if they have feedback on a particular guideline, or if they would like to suggest changes or additions to guidelines.

### Next version

If you have a date when you expect an updated version of guidelines to come out, you may want to include that in your guidelines.

### A cover page

Consider creating your own cover page if you can make it colorful and attractive. That will attract people's interest in picking up and looking at your guidelines book.

# Who to Involve

In order for guidelines to be successful people must buy in to them. The best way for people to buy into guidelines is to be involved in the process. The most successful guidelines implementation strategies come from involving people at two levels:

- ❑ A core-group level
- ❑ Reviewer level

## Core group

Your core group of guidelines task force members should be around six to eight people, and they should be representative of both developers and user groups within business units. This core group is responsible for:

- ❑ Making any changes to customize the guidelines.
- ❑ Developing a rollout and implementation plan.
- ❑ Implementing the rollout plan.
- ❑ Deciding who should be the guidelines coordinator for maintenance and updating.

The amount of time the core group puts in on the guidelines project and how long they need to be together depends on the extent of customization you are doing. It is typical for core-group members to put in three to six hours per week for four to six weeks to customize and roll out guidelines. This is an average, since some weeks are busier than others.

## The reviewer group

In addition to the six to eight core-group members, you should decide on a larger group of reviewer members. You may have anywhere from eight to twenty members in your reviewer group.

The more people you have, the more work you have, but the more buy-in you have. The reviewer group members have the following responsibilities:

- ❑ Reviewing drafts of a customized document.
- ❑ Reviewing rollout plans and make comments.
- ❑ Getting the word out when guidelines are available.

Reviewer group members can expect to spend about two hours a week for about four weeks. This is a great role for people to play who are critical in the buy-in process.

## Project Planning for Customizing Guidelines

Here are some milestone points in a guidelines plan. You should adjust these to best fit your own process, but this list will act as a starting point for you to plan out your guidelines project.

### Initial steps

- ❑ Decide who will be in the core group.
- ❑ Decide who will be in the reviewer group.
- ❑ Have all core-group members review this guidelines document.

### Have a kick-off meeting

Have a kick-off meeting to decide the following:

- ❑ Scope of guidelines
- ❑ General process milestone dates
- ❑ Roles and responsibilities
- ❑ Required time commitment
- ❑ Suggestions for reviewer group that have not been completed

### Assign a task force coordinator

It is the coordinator's job to get all the information out to everyone, confirm meetings, take notes, and so on.

### Assign research jobs

Decide how you want to proceed with customization decisions. Consider assigning different jobs to different people or teams on your core group.

For example, you may want to split your core group into three groups of two.

- ❑ Assign different topics to teams for researching customization decisions.
- ❑ Another team might be responsible for coming up with the initial roll-out plan.

Often guidelines task forces will divide up this book and have each team come back to the group with suggestions for customization.

Once you have agreed upon what customization you are going to do, assign rewriting, rewording, and taking new screen pictures. Creating and shooting screen pictures is probably the most time-consuming part of the project. If you give a person or a team this responsibility, make sure they have plenty of help and time to do it.

### Research media decisions

Have one team check out your options for creating the document.

- ❑ Who is designing and printing the cover page?
- ❑ Are you printing a hard copy?
- ❑ What tools will you use to take screen captures?
- ❑ Will the paper document use color?

❑ What kind of bindings will you use?

❑ How much printing lead time do you need?

❑ What tools will you use to put the document online?

### Create a new draft

Once you have gathered all the customized changes, create a new draft of the guidelines.

### Send the draft out to reviewers

This is when your draft goes to the reviewer group. Make sure you give them instructions as to what you want them to do.

Some suggestions might be to have them identify any guidelines they find hard to understand or would be hard to implement. You may want to suggest to them that you are going to listen carefully to all their suggestions, although you may not be able to implement them all immediately.

### Get feedback and decide what to act on

Once you get feedback from your core group and your reviewer group on the draft, you need to decide what changes you are actually going to implement and then make them.

## Rolling Out and Implementing Guidelines

In order for your guidelines to be successful, people must know they exist and be encouraged to use them. As early in the process as possible, you should put together a roll-out and implementation plan to identify how you are going to announce and get guidelines out. Companies who succeed in implementing guidelines effectively are companies who plan the introduction of the guidelines.

The particular methods you use to roll out guidelines need to be customized to your own corporate culture. As a starting point, think about how change has occurred successfully in your organization in the past. If there have been recent ways of rolling out new technologies or new ideas, you may want to copy the methods used. Do not let all the hard work in getting your customized guidelines out the door flop because no one knew or got excited about their birth.

Below are some ideas for you to think about in putting together your own rollout and implementation plan.

## Announce the guidelines

### Create an event

People will notice that guidelines are out if there is an event surrounding them. These events can take many forms. In order for people to receive their copy of guidelines or their ID for signing on to an online guidelines document, they would need to attend one of the following events:

- ❑ A brief five-to-ten minute meeting with the guidelines coordinator explaining what they are, how to use them, and who to contact for more information.

- ❑ A one-hour, half-day, or one-day class on the guidelines themselves, or an announcement at a group meeting, at a project level, department level or company-wide level.

### Posters

Some companies have successfully announced guidelines with the use of posters on bulletin boards and elevators.

### E-mail

Announce that guidelines are out and available under your e-mail system.

### Project-level meetings

Schedule meetings with each GUI project team and distribute the guidelines at these meetings.

### In combination with training

If you have a training class scheduled for a related purpose, such as GUI design or a programming-tool class, you may want to consider announcing and handing out guidelines at that event.

### Design contest

Some companies have someone very high up in the organization sponsor a GUI design contest. Any project teams who have developed a new application or part of an application that follows the new guidelines is eligible to participate in the GUI design contest. You then announce finalists and the winner with the best application.

### Don't forget your users

Make sure you include your user community in the roll out. They need to know about the guidelines, too.

## Assign a guidelines coordinator

As soon as guidelines are announced you must immediately be ready to answer questions and concerns about them.

Make sure you have at least one person who is designated as the guidelines coordinator. This person takes calls and answers questions about particular guidelines and implementation.

If you have an interface design specialist, that is a good person to appoint guidelines coordinator, since the guidelines coordinator is often in the role of helping people change and adjust their interfaces to conform to guidelines.

### Decide where guidelines fit

You will need to decide ahead of time where guidelines fit in your organization. Are they enforced, and if so who does the enforcing, and how is the enforcement going to take place? Are they suggestions only, and if so, who is responsible for promoting them?

Many developers will welcome using guidelines if they can get help early on in applying them. If you have an existing standards committee, you may want that group to take over the role or be involved in some way in the application of the new GUI guidelines.

Make sure that you have ironed out everyone's roles and responsibilities before the guidelines are widely distributed.

### Consider starting with a paper copy

The most successful implementation of guidelines starts with a hard-cover book before or in addition to an online document. Although there are many advantages to online documents (access, easy to update), experience has shown that it is critical to have a book to wave in your hand and bring to meetings when you are first implementing GUI guidelines. Consider using a book, at least to start, and moving to an online document at a later time.

### Binding

The best binding method for a hard-cover book of this kind is a plastic spiral. This is not a GBC binding. A GBC-type binding cannot be turned all the way around and laid flat on a desk. Plastic spiral bindings can be bent all the way around. They are actually more durable than metal spiral, which is second best.

Resist the urge to print your hard copy guidelines in a loose-leaf notebook format thinking it will allow you to update them easily. Updating such documents is a nightmare. Although it may seem like you are saving money by not having to reprint the whole book, you will find that you will actually spend much more money for the following reasons:

- ❑ Most of the book is probably going to have to be reprinted anyway as soon as the page numbers change.

- ❑ People will never update their hard-copy books; after a while, no one will be working from the current version.

- ❑ Binders cost more than plastic spiral.

## Maintaining and updating your guidelines

You should go into guidelines implementation with the assumption that the guidelines will need to be updated. As your GUI applications mature you may want to add more button names, new screen examples, and other modifications to reflect your changing designs.

### Allow exceptions

Effective guidelines are designed to fit 80 percent of the time. That means you must assume that there are some places where some people will need exceptions. There are three ways that you can handle requests for exceptions. When someone comes to you and tells you that they cannot follow a particular guideline because it's contrary to what the users want in their application, you can:

- ❑ Show them how they can follow guidelines and still meet user requirements.

- ❑ Grant them an exception.

- ❑ Do either of the above, plus make note of the exception for the future.

When many development groups request the same exception, that means that particular guideline is not working in your organization, and you need to consider changing it in the next release.

### Strategies for updating your guidelines

As soon as guidelines are rolled out, you should begin to maintain a list of changes, suggestions for changes, and requested exceptions. Keep a file with all of the changes that people suggest. Decide ahead of time who will maintain this file, who is responsible for it, and what the criteria are for doing a new release of guidelines to incorporate these changes.

For example, you may set a time period where six months from the day the guidelines are first rolled out you will begin Release Two. How quickly you need to consider a next release depends on how much change is going on in your GUI programming projects. If there are likely to be many tool changes, staff changes, and many new applications, you will likely need a new release soon. Three-to-six months is a typical time frame for a second release to fine tune the first guidelines.

### Putting guidelines online

In the long run, you should consider having an online document in addition to, or in place of a hard copy document. Your guidelines will be easier to update and maintain in online format.

The guidelines in this package you have purchased are available in an online format or you can convert your own guidelines to an online document file in Windows using several utility packages that make the conversion from Word to Windows help relatively easy and quick.

# A

# Appendix

# List of Guidelines

*The following pages list all the guidelines, by chapter and topic within each chapter.*

## Contents

Controls

Data Fields

Dialog Boxes and Windows

Menus

Messages

Color

Icons and Toolbars

Metaphors

Fonts

Visual Coding

Graphing

Navigation and Interaction

Online Help

## Chapter 1 Controls

 *Push Buttons*

Use only for frequent or critical immediate actions
Label push buttons carefully
Label consistently
Use industry standards for labels
Consider replacing the OK button with a specific term
Size buttons relative to each other
Separate buttons from the rest of the window
Group buttons together
Place buttons consistently
Match button position to the use of the window
Position limited action push buttons where needed
Order buttons consistently
Use chevrons (>>) to imply an expanding dialog box
Use ellipses (...) to imply an additional dialog box
Use graying out to show unavailability
Assign a nondestructive default button

### Radio Buttons

Use radio buttons for one choice
Label radio buttons descriptively
Group radio buttons together and label them
Align radio buttons vertically
Limit radio buttons to six or less
Choose an order
Avoid binary radio buttons

### Check Boxes

Use check boxes for choosing more than one option
Use check boxes for toggling
Label check boxes descriptively

Group and label check boxes
Align check boxes vertically
Limit check boxes to ten or fewer
Choose an order
Do not use Select all or Deselect all check boxes
Use check boxes in place of binary radio buttons

## List Boxes

Use list boxes for long lists
Use list boxes for dynamic data
Show three-to-eight items at a time
Label each list box
Use filters for large lists
Use drop-down list boxes to save space
Use a combination list box to allow users to type in an option
Use a multiple-select list box instead of check boxes
Consider instructions for multiple-select list boxes
Show pick results in a summary box
Consider Select All or Deselect All buttons

## Spin Boxes

Use spin boxes for limited cycling
Combine spin boxes with data-entry fields

## Sliders

Use sliders for visually choosing values
Use sliders for large data ranges
Display results
Allow data entry
Allow the use of arrows for small increments

## Drag and Drop

Consider drag-and-drop interaction
Avoid a single use of drag and drop
Use visual feedback

# Chapter 2 Data Fields

### Presenting and Entering Data

Place a box around data-entry fields

Show display-only data without a box

Use a graying out for temporarily protected fields

Use the box length to signify data length

Match the lengths of data boxes

Align data fields

Group data fields

### Data-Field Labels

Label all data fields

Place labels to the left

Align data-entry labels to the left

Place a colon after data labels

# Chapter 3 Dialog Boxes and Windows

### Presentation of Windows and Dialog Boxes

Use cascading windows

Avoid horizontal scrolling

Use expanding dialogs

Size secondary windows to fit data

Place pop-ups in the center of the action

Use modal dialogs for closure

Use modeless dialogs for continuing work

### Navigation and Order

Organize windows and dialogs to match work flow

Use an appropriate amount of information

Find a home

Organize information within a window

Choose a horizontal or vertical flow

Group similar data

Minimize different margins

Some general guidelines

# Chapter 4 Menus

### Designing Effective Menus

Word menu items carefully

Change menus as you need to

Use initial caps

Follow industry standards

### Menu Bars

Match menu bars to the users' work flow

Give critical or frequent tasks even weight

Place application-specific menu items where they fit

Replace the word File if necessary

Use one word only for menu-bar items

Use only one line for the menus

Do not gray out menu-bar items

### Pull-Downs

Use more than one pull-down item

Use unique pull-down items

Use up to one screen length of pull-downs

Put frequent or important items at the top

Use separator bars

Use no more than two levels of cascading

Use ellipses (...) to denote dialogs

Use industry-standard keyboard equivalents

Use accelerators sparingly

Use consistent accelerators

### Special Menus

Use pop-up menus for specific options

Consider using roll-up menus

# Chapter 5 Messages

### Presenting Messages

Use messages when and where they are needed

Place messages in the center of the current activity

### Wording

Be descriptive

Use active voice

Use terms the users understand

Avoid humor and humanizing

### Different Message Types

Use information messages for results

Use warning messages for critical confirmations

Use critical messages for system errors

Use in-progress messages for waits

### Error Messages

Use three critical pieces of information

Don't blame users

Use Help on error messages

Avoid negative wording

### Feedback and In-Progress Messages

Use two critical pieces of information for feedback

Inform users how long the wait will be

Show progress status visually

## Chapter 6 Color

### Using Color

Use color to get attention

Use color sparingly

Limit colors to three per screen

Combine color with redundant highlighting

Watch out for color blindness

Watch out for color customizing

Consider the restrictions of monochrome monitors

Use colors consistently

Use color in icons sparingly

### Color Choices and Combinations

Follow cultural color meanings

Use light backgrounds for main areas

Avoid red-and-blue combinations

Avoid deep blue for backgrounds

Avoid blue text

Use enough contrast

Avoid light text on dark

Use grayware first

### Color in Graphs and Charts

Use primary colors to show differences

Avoid red

Use close colors to show transition

Use light backgrounds for tables

### User Customizing

Let users customize
Use color palettes
Provide a reset
Show results before setting

## Chapter 7 Icons and Toolbars

### When to Use Icons

Use icons for a purpose
Use button images as shortcuts
Use icons when a picture is worth . . .
Use icons for international use

### Designing or Choosing Pictures

Decide on an approach
Develop a cohesive set
Include just enough detail for recognition
Use standard pictures
Consider changing the button image's state
Test your images

### Using Pictures in the Interface

Be consistent
Avoid words
Watch out for international meanings

### Toolbars

Use toolbars for frequent actions across screens
Use toolbars to supplement menus
Use toolbars in place of some menu items
Make toolbars consistent

Make only active items available
Allow users to move some toolbars
Allow users to toggle toolbars on and off
Allow customizing
Use white space for grouping
Limit button images to 15

## Chapter 8 Metaphors

### Use an Appropriate Metaphor

Consider using metaphors
Use industry-standard metaphors if they fit
Only use a metaphor within the users' world
Choose metaphors carefully
Make sure metaphors work together
Choose a metaphor that fits the task
Use the metaphor consistently
Don't rely on pictures alone
Extend the metaphor if you need to
Explain the metaphors
Test your metaphors
Avoid being unique

## Chapter 9 Fonts

### Using Fonts Effectively

Use a sans serif font
Do not use italics or underlining
Avoid using colored fonts
Use bold for emphasis

Avoid changing font size
Use 10- and 12-point fonts
Minimize the number of different fonts

# Chapter 10 Visual Coding

## Using Visual Coding Effectively

Use visual coding for meaning
Use graying out for unavailability
Use graying out for items that do not need attention
Use reverse video for high attention
Use bold for items that need attention
Use boxes or borders to group or get attention
Use all caps only for emphasis
Avoid blinking

# Chapter 11 Graphing

## When to Use Graphs

Use graphs for relationships
Use tables for specific values

## Designing a Graph

Use bar graphs for categories
Use special effects carefully
Use a pie chart for part-to-whole relationships
Use line charts for continuous data
Choose appropriate scales
Consider displaying specific values
Use visual coding on graphs

Use legends for complicated graphs

Label graphs and data

## Chapter 12 Navigation and Interaction

### Making Navigation Decisions

Match the users' work flow

Choose and show an obvious path

Use an appropriate unit of work

Find a home

### Pointing Devices and Keyboard Support

Provide support for both pointing and keyboard

Design for one device

Consider right-mouse clicks

## Chapter 13 Online Help

### What to Put Online

Use help for the right kind of information

Know your platform

Consider user needs

Put online

Don't put online

### Writing for Online

Use documentation professionals

Decide how much paper you will provide

Diagram the entire help system before writing

Limit the number of heading levels

Keep text concise

Keep topics short

Create standalone chunks

Design for access

Organize information for quick access and comprehension

Be consistent

Use active voice

Use present tense

Use the informal pronoun *you*

Write effective procedures

How to make a help file

## Windows and Pop-ups

Understand how each Windows display type works

Use different Windows display types for specific information

## Main Contents Window

Include the following types of topic titles

Design the main contents window

Consider using graphics

Use pull-down menus

Provide a unique mnemonic

## Button Bar

Use the button bar for continual access to actions or topics

Use standard Windows buttons

Create new buttons

## Links

Link your application to help

Link topics together

Create pop-ups for terms in the topics

Use graphics as hotspots

Plan your index carefully

Link files to other files within a help system

Connect one help system to another help system

Link help systems to external programs

Limit the number of hotspots

## Context-Sensitive Help

Use map numbers to link the application to the help file

You can use several help files

## Glossaries

Multiple glossaries

Use alphabetical buttons

Avoid coding a glossary term too often

## Keyword Search

Allow enough time

How it works

Think like your users

Be selective in your indexing

Nest index terms

Use synonyms

Maintain a list of words you are indexing

Understand your tool

Control topic titles

Test your index

## Navigation

Don't let users get lost

Allow users to move up the hierarchy

## Screen Images and Graphics

Use images of screens judiciously

Use a screen-grab program

Use monochrome images
Clean up your images
Do not scale bitmapped images
Place bitmaps by reference
Answer these questions before adding graphics

## Color

Use color for substantive reasons only
Consider these problems
Use no more than three colors
Do not use color alone to cue readers
Use color consistently
Use familiar color codes
Test your use of color
Follow industry standards to code hotspots

## Testing

Test the entire file thoroughly

## Conventions

Check recent commercial help systems
Capitalization
Fonts for different text
Type characteristics
Tables
Unsupported characters

# B

## *For More Information*

*Following are lists of selected reference materials and resource organizations.*

### Contents

## Interface Design

Galitz, Wilbert O. *It's Time to Clean Your Windows: Designing GUIs that Work*. John Wiley & Sons, 1994.

Heckel, Paul. *The Elements of Friendly Software Design*. Sybix, 1991.

Helander, Martin, editor. *Handbook of Human-Computer Interaction*. North Holland, 1988.

Horton, William. *The Icon Book*. John Wiley & Sons, 1994.

Laurel, Brenda. *The Art of Human-Computer Interface Design*. Addison-Wesley, 1990.

Marcus, Aaron. *Graphic Design for Electronic Documents and User Interfaces*. ACM Press, 1992.

Mayhew, Deborah. *Software User Interface Design*. Prentice-Hall, Inc., 1992.

Schneiderman, Ben. *Designing the User Interface*. Addison-Wesley, 1992.

Sullivan, Joseph, and Sherman Tyler, editors. *Intelligent User Interfaces*. Addison-Wesley, 1992.

Tognazzini, Bruce "Tog." *TOG on Interface*. Addison-Wesley, 1992.

White, Jan. *Color for the Electronic Age*. Watson Guptill, 1990.

## Human Factors Engineering

Norman, Don. *The Design of Everyday Things*. Basic Books, 1988.

Norman, Don. *Things That Make Us Smart*. Addison-Wesley, 1992.

Norman, Don. *Turn Signals Are the Facial Expressions of Automobiles*. Addison-Wesley, 1992.

## Conceptual Design/Work Flow Analysis

Bauersfeld, Penny. *Software By Design*, MT Books, 1994.

Greenbaum, J. and M. Kyng, editors. *Design at Work*. Erlbaum, 1991.

Martin, C. *User-Centered Requirements Analysis*. Prentice-Hall, 1988.

Namioka, A. and D. Schuler, editors. *Participatory Design: Principles and Practice*. Erlbaum, 1993.

## Platform Guidelines

Kobara, Shiz. *Visual Design with OSF/Motif*. Addison-Wesley, 1991.

*Macintosh Human Interface Guidelines*. Apple Computer, 1992.

*Object-Oriented Interface Design, IBM Common User Access Guidelines*. IBM, QUE, December 1992.

*Open Look Graphical User Interface Application Style Guidelines*. Sun Microsystems, Inc., 1991.

*OSF/Motif Programmer's Guide and OSF/Motif Style Guide*. Prentice-Hall, 1991.

*The Windows Interface: An Application Design Guide*. Microsoft, 1992.

## Online Help and Documentation

Boggan, Scott, David Farkas, and Joe Welinski. *Developing Online Help for Windows*. Sams, 1993.

Gery, Gloria. *EPSS*. Weingarten Publications, 1992.

Horton, William O. *Designing and Writing Online Documentation*, 2nd Ed., John Wiley & Sons, 1994.

Horton, William O. *Illustrating Computer Documentation*. John Wiley & Sons, 1994.

Kearsley, Greg. *On-Line Help Systems*. Ablex Publishing Corp., 1988.

Mischel, Jim, and Jeff Duntemann. *The Developers Guide to WINHELP.EZE, Harnessing the Windows Help Engine*. John Wiley & Sons, 1994.

"The Encyclopedic Reference as Model for Print Documentation," *Technical Communication*, Second Quarter, 1990.

## Usability Testing

Nielsen, Jacob, and Robert L. Mack, editors. *Usability Inspection Methods*. John Wiley & Sons, 1994.

Redish, Janice C., and Joseph S. Duma. *A Practical Usability Testing*. Ablex Publishing, 1993.

Rubin, Jeffrey. *Handbook of Usability Testing: How to Plan, Design, and Conduct Effective Tests*. John Wiley & Sons, 1994.

## Resources

### Compuserve

The Windows SDK (Software Development Kit) Forum, GO WINSDK, has a section (16) on WINHELP/TOOLS. Also look in section 4 of WINAPD (Windows Third Party Applications D Forum).

### Human Factors and Ergonomics Society

PO Box 1369
Santa Monica, CA 90406-1369
Phone:    310-394-1811
Fax:        310-394-2410

### Internet

There is an interface design news group found at:
comp.human-factors.

The WinHelp Newsgroup can be found at:
comp.os.ms-windows.programmer.winhlp.

You can subscribe to the WinHelp Mail List by sending the following unsigned e-mail message on the Internet:

Address:    listserv@admin.humberc.on.ca
Message:    sub winhlp-L

**SIGCHI** (Special Interest Group for Computer Human Interaction)

Association for Computing Machinery
11 West 42nd Street
New York, NY 10036
Phone:    212-869-7440

## Society for Technical Communication

901 N. Stuart St., Suite 904
Arlington, VA 22203-1854
Phone:    703-522-4114
Fax:      703-522-2075
BBS:      703-522-3299

## Usability Professionals Association

Sandi Erspamer
10875 Plano Road
Suite 115
Dallas, TX 75238
Phone:    214-349-8841
Fax:      214-349-7946

# Appendix C

# Working with the Files

## Contents

## Before You Begin

### How to Use the Customization guide

1. Decide if you will be distributing the customized guidelines only online, only on paper, or both online and on paper.
2. Read the *Before you Begin* section.
3. Know your tools thoroughly.
4. Read the *Global Features* section.
5. Read the *Online*, *Paper Deliverable*, or *From Paper to Online* sections, depending on your decision in step one.

### Paper or Online?

You should decide if you want to distribute your guidelines as a paper document, online, or both. The files included in this package were optimized to function as online help, so while they make an acceptable paper document, if this is to be your primary distribution medium you may want to make some changes. See the *Paper Deliverable* section for suggestions.

### Review the Instructions

Look through this guide and be sure you understand all the Microsoft Word for Windows features used to create the manual. You will need to understand and be familiar with advanced Word features.

### Know Your Tools

Understand your tools, both Word and the tool you use to create online help.

This manual does not attempt to teach you how to use your tools. Use your manual, online help, or a third-party reference.

## Software Used to Prepare the Files

The GUI Guidelines book was prepared using Microsoft Word for Windows 6.0a. Doc-To-Help 1.6 (Wextech) was used to convert the text files to online help.

Screen images were grabbed from their applications and then cleaned up in Microsoft Paintbrush.

## References to Menu Options and Commands

Instructions to select options from Word's toolbars and menus are presented with hyphens between each selection. For instance, File-Print-Current Page indicates that you select File from the menu bar, and then select Print from the pull-down menu. In the dialog box that appears, click on Current Page.

## Safety Points

### Make a set of backup files

Duplicate all the original files and keep them in a safe place. Do not make any changes to the original files. You may need to go back to them if something goes wrong with the files you are modifying.

### Save your work often as you go

Make frequent backups of your work as you make changes. It is not unusual when using advanced features to have your system lock up or fail. You do not want to lose hours of work.

### If you have memory or performance problems

- ❏ Do not use Allow Fast Saves.
- ❏ Place all graphics as pictures.

❏ Close all other open applications and documents.

❏ Use normal view, not page layout view.

❏ Refer to *Optimizing Word* in the Word manual.

❏ Save all files, exit your applications, and exit Windows. Then start Windows and open only the applications you need for this work.

See *Doc-To-Help and memory*, on page 196.

### Turn off Allow Fast Saves

Turn off Word's save feature called Allow Fast Saves. You will find this under Tools-Options-Save. This feature causes the files to be larger than if you use a regular save.

### Consider breaking up the text file into smaller units

To make it easier for writers who are not experienced with Word, Doc-To-Help, or other help tools, both the .DOC and the .RTF files contain all the GUI guidelines contents. While it is easier to work with one file, it is very time consuming. Also, the size of the files will strain Window's system resources and your RAM. You may want to break the book into separate files for each chapter. If you decide to do this, read the manuals for your software for the best techniques.

## Getting Started

### *How to Install and Use the Disk Files*

### Files you have received

You have received one CD with this customization guide. This CD has the online help files for the GUI Guidelines manual. These files are ready to use after installation.

❏ .HLP is the basic online help file.

❏ .DHN provides the Navigator for online help.

❑ .DOC is a text file. Use this to create paper documents or if you are using Doc-To-Help.

❑ .RTF is a text file ready for the help compiler. It can be used with any online help tool.

❑ .HPJ is the help project file.

## About the Software

### What You'll Need

To run the help files and use the customizable files you will need a PC environment.

### For the help files:

❑ IBM PC or compatible

❑ CD-ROM player

❑ Windows 3.1 or later

### For the customizable files:

❑ IBM PC compatible with at least 8MB of RAM and 20MB of free space on a hard drive

❑ CD-ROM player

❑ Windows 3.1 or higher

❑ Word for Windows 6.0a to create paper documents

❑ A Windows help authoring tool (Doc-to-Help or RoboHelp, for example) to create a modified help file

### About the Software

There are two distinct sets of files loaded on the CD-ROM:

**Help files:**  The files required to display the GUI Guidelines found in the book as Windows online help.

**Customizable files:**  The source files for the online help. These can be modified to create your own version of the help files.

The following table lists all of the files in alphabetical order, indicates whether they are part of the help files or customizable files, and what each file contains. Copy the customization files to your hard drive, all in the same directory.

| *File* | *File Set* | *Purpose* | *Install on hard drive* |
|---|---|---|---|
| d2hlink.dll | Help | Help system file | |
| d2hnav.exe | Help | Doc-To-Help Navigator Application | |
| d2hnav.hlp | Help | Help for the Doc-To-Help Navigator Application | |
| doc2help.inf | Customize | Doc-To-Help file | Yes |
| doc2help.ini | Customize | Doc-To-Help file | Yes |
| guiohw.dhn | Help | Doc-To-Help Navigator file | |
| guiohw.doc | Customize | Word for Windows text file | Yes |
| guiohw.hlp | Help | Actual Help file | |
| guiohw.hpj | Customize | Help project file | Yes |
| guiohw.rtf | Customize | RTF file for the Word text file | Yes |
| msoutlin.vbx | Help | Help system file | |

## Installing the Software

To install the software, follow these simple steps:

1. Start Windows on your computer.
2. Place the CD-ROM into your CD-ROM drive.
3. From Program Manager, Select File, **Run**, and type **X:\INSTALL** (where "X" is the correct letter of your CD-ROM drive).
4. Follow the screen prompts to complete the installation.

The installation program copies two files to your WINDOWS directory, and two files to your WINDOWS/SYSTEM directory. You will need the CD-ROM to run the application provided.

### User Assistance and Information

John Wiley & Sons, Inc. is pleased to provided assistance to users of this CD-ROM. Should you have questions regarding the installation or use of this package, please call our technical support number at (212) 850-6194 weekdays between 9 AM and 4 PM EST.

To place orders for additional copies of this book or software, or to request information about other Wiley products, please call (800) 879-4539, on email at compbks@jwiley.com, or use the business-reply card found in the back of this book.

| *Note* |
| --- |
| If you are installing this to a LAN or if your Windows files are on a LAN, the install program may not be able to create a program group window for you in Program Manager. If this occurs you will get an error message. You should still be able to run the help files by going to File Manager, finding the GUI1.HLP file, and double-clicking on it. |

### Setting up the Templates

If you are using Doc-To-Help to modify files for help or for paper and help, be sure that the templates D2H_NORM.DOT and D2H_HELP.DOT are installed either in your Word template directory or in the directory with the files. Use File-Templates to attach the D2H_NORM.DOT template to the .DOC file.

If you are using another online help tool, check the instructions for any special template requirements.

## Global Features

### Introduction

The information in this section applies whether you will distribute the document on paper or online. Follow these conventions to maintain consistency through the entire document.

### Redundancy in the GUI Guidelines Manual

Each chapter in the guidelines addresses a different interface element. Redundancy is included so that readers do not have to flip from one section to another. For example, a guideline will be repeated in both *Push Buttons* and in *Radio Buttons* if it applies to both elements.

### Spelling

These words are spelled as follows:

bitmap
check box
combination list box
context-sensitive
display-only
drag-and-drop
drop-down
feedback
gray out
hotspots
in-progress
laptop

list box

menu items

menu bar

multiple-select

nonscrolling

OK (the button)

okay (the word)

online

pop-up

pull-down

push button

radio button

screen-grab

single-select

spin box

standalone

toolbar

### Capitalization

All guidelines (Heading 3s) are formatted in *downstyle*. Downstyle is a method of capitalization in which only the first word of a heading and proper nouns are capitalized.

Headings 1 and 2 have initial capitalization—all main words are capitalized.

### Change Text

- ❑ Type over, add, or delete text as you wish.

- ❑ Be careful to apply or maintain the correct styles.

- ❑ Do not type an extra hard return at ends of lines or paragraphs to create space. The space is built into the styles.

### *Guidelines*

Guidelines are statements about the use of a specific GUI feature. They are formatted as Heading 3 and have no end punctuation.

- ❑ Required guidelines are followed by a checkmark.
- ❑ Optional guidelines do not have a checkmark.

The simplest way to create a new required guideline heading is to copy another one and paste it where you want the new guideline. Then just type over the existing text.

### Subheadings under a guideline

Subpoints of a guideline are usually formatted as Heading 4. Avoid using a fourth heading level unless it is necessary to break up a large block of text to make it easier for users to scan for their information.

In this file, Heading 4 is used to identify platform-based examples. This optimizes the file for online help. If your primary delivery media is paper you may want to make some design changes in this area.

### *References*

References to books, chapters, and sections in chapters appear in italics.

### *Viewing Special Text*

Many of the codes used to create Word files are not visible when you view the document in a normal way.

### Fields

Fields are a form of programming code that tells Word to do certain things with your document, such as build a cross-reference, index a term, create a table of contents, or add a heading title to a footer. They are a very powerful feature; if you are not familiar with them read a manual or the online help. You can see a list of them under Insert-Field.

### Field states

Fields are either codes or results.

Table of contents field code as a formula: {·TOC·\o·"2-2"·}

Table of contents field as results:

| Presenting·data | → | 38¶ |
|---|---|---|
| Data·field·labels | → | 40¶ |

### Viewing field codes/field results

There are two ways to view field codes or their results.

1. Select Tools-Options-View-Field Codes. All fields will be seen as codes (formulas) rather than as normal text (results).

2. Position your cursor inside a field. Press the right mouse button and select Toggle Field Codes from the menu.

---

**Note:**

To make field codes gray, select Tools-Options-View and make a choice from the Field Shading list box.

Example of gray field: Presenting data

---

### Hidden text

Some field codes, such as index codes, are formatted as hidden text. They can only be seen when you have chosen to view hidden text. Select Tools-Options-View-Hidden Text to see them or toggle them on and off by pressing the Show/Hide button on the button bar. ¶

### Footers

To view the footers without having access to changing them, select Page Layout view. Scroll down until the footer appears. It will be in gray, indicating that you cannot change it at this time.

To view and change footers, select View-Header and Footer. Then click on the toggle button, the first button on the button bar. Toggle the field codes on and off to see the codes and the results.

### *Pictures*

To speed up scrolling through the document, pictures are often displayed as empty boxes. To toggle this feature on and off, select Tools-Options-View-Picture Placeholders.

## Online Help

### *Introduction*

The information in this section covers what you need to do to modify the files to create online help. If you will be creating a paper version of the guidelines in addition or instead of paper, see that section of this appendix.

Although these files were created using Doc-To-Help, you can use any online help tool to modify them and then regenerate the help file. These instructions will be generic when they refer to tools, so be familiar with the tool you are using.

### *Know Your Tools*

Understand your tools.

- ❑ Know the effects of changing text in a heading.
- ❑ Know how to alter or create keyword search (index) entries.
- ❑ Know how to change the perceived order of topics and the browse sequences.
- ❑ Know how to add or alter hypertext links.

### Directories and Files

You must store the .RTF files and the .HPJ files in the same directory. Bitmaps should be stored in a BITMAPS subdirectory to this directory.

### Change Text

Change the text and guidelines to fit your corporation. As you do this,

❑ Be careful not to change styles.

❑ Use the same styles for new information as used for similar types of information (guideline sentence, text) in the existing book.

### Headings for Subtopic Jumps

Text to introduce a list of jumps to other topics can say whatever you want. Find the text inserted by the software (in your file it is coded RelatedHead) and change it to fit the specific information at each location.

### Bullets

The help compiler cannot handle unusual bullets. You should create them as follows:

1. Position the cursor where you want the bullet.
2. Select List style.
3. Type Alt-0183. Num Lock must be on.
4. Press the Tab key.
5. Highlight the bullet and format it as Symbol font, 10 points.

The easiest way to do this is to just copy an existing bullet and paste it in the new position.

## Doc-To-Help and Memory

If you are using Doc-To-Help as your online tool, you will need to do the following to avoid Out of Memory messages during the Make Into Help process.

In addition to the suggestions on pages 185–86, do the following:

- ❏ Select normal view.
- ❏ Select 75 percent view.
- ❏ Check the minimize box in the Reformat as Help File dialog box.
- ❏ Run Make into Help conversions in steps.

### To run Make into Help in steps:

1. Starting with the .DOC file, select Format-Make into Help.
2. When the following dialog box appears, turn off all the conversions except the first two, Preliminary Reformatting and Create Contents Topic.

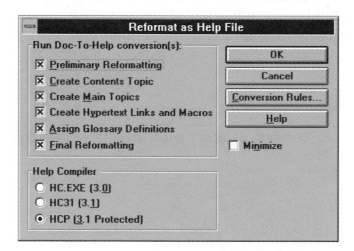

After these two conversions are complete, you will be in the .RTF file.

3. In the .RTF file, start with the first conversion not checked above, Create Main Topics. Check only this conversion, check Minimize, and then OK.

4. Repeat step 3 for the remaining conversions, one at a time.

### Time

Depending on the speed of your machine, it may take several hours to do the entire Make into Help and Compile process.

### The Navigator

Doc-To-Help has a feature called *Navigator* that allows the users to see an outline of all the topics while they work, and allows a Parent Topic button to move them up the topic hierarchy easily. The online help files distributed with this package use the Navigator. If you want this feature, you must use Doc-To-Help.

If you change the order, add, or delete headings you must refresh the topic list in the Navigator and recompile the file.

If you do not use the Doc-To-Help and the Navigator, be sure to remove the Navigator and Parent Topic buttons from the button bar in the help file.

### Indexing

Test the keyword search in the current file with your users. Note any problems they have finding information and then add or change index entries.

In the .RTF file, keywords (index terms) are stored in the footer. Understand how your tool works so that you can add or change keywords.

### Graphics

Do not scale graphics in Word. Scale .BMP images in a draw program and then cut and paste them into Word.

Be sure that your screen images do *not* have a heading style applied to them.

## Paper Deliverable

### *Introduction*

The .DOC files you will be using have been optimized for online use. You can use them as is, but you will have a more usable paper document if you make some changes. Some of these changes are easy, but some will require advanced Microsoft Word skills.

If you are intending to deliver the guidelines on both paper and online, read both this section and *From Paper to Online*. If you want to maintain a single source file, you will need to be familiar with all the sections of this chapter. You should use, and thoroughly understand, Doc-To-Help.

### *Learn about Word features*

You will need to be comfortable with all basic Word features. In addition, be sure you understand:

- ❑ Templates
- ❑ Styles
- ❑ Field codes
- ❑ Footers
- ❑ Sections

### *The GUI Guidelines Template*

The .DOC file was created using the Doc-To-Help D2H_NORM.DOT template. However, the NORMAL.DOT template was attached to the file so that you would not have to have Doc-To-Help to modify the file in Word.

If you keep the file attached to the NORMAL.DOT template it will function, but you should know that all the styles in the document are stored only in the document, not in the template.

You can follow Word instructions to create a unique template for this document if you wish.

You can use the .DOC file as delivered, with the NORMAL.DOT template attached. The styles will work, as will the keyboard short-cuts that make applying styles quicker. See Format-Style-Modify-Shortcut Key to see what keyboard combination is assigned to a style.

## Page Setup

Go to File-Page Setup to verify or modify the settings. The documents were all prepared with the following settings.

### Margins

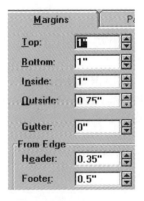

### Paper size

### Layout

This layout applies to each section. Word will automatically insert a blank page before each new section if it is required to force the next section to start on an odd page.

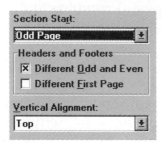

## *Adding and Deleting Chapters*

If you add a chapter, put it in its own section. Make the section settings as shown in Page Setup.

If you increase file size by adding information without deleting any, you may want to break the file into individual files, one for each chapter, to reduce the demand for system resources and memory.

If you delete a chapter, be sure to delete its section break.

## *Breaking up the File*

If you decide to break up the single file into multiple files, you must thoroughly understand how to work with multiple files in Word. Read the appropriate section of the manual. Following are some suggestions:

❑ Do not use the Master Document feature to link the files. Use the older method of RD codes. Refer to a manual for Word 2.0 for assistance.

❑ Do not rename a file after creating the RD fields or the master document.

❑ Be sure you keep all files in the same directory. If you make files for the table of contents and index, they also must be in this directory.

## *Templates and Styles*

### What is included in a style

Every paragraph and graphic in Word has a style attached to it. Styles contain the name and size of the font used in that style. In addition, the following can be included in a style:

❑ Type appearance, like bold or italics
❑ Indentation
❑ Space above and below a paragraph
❑ Space between lines of text

Please review Format-Font and Format-Paragraph for a more complete understanding of what can be included in a style.

Styles are stored in templates.

### Understand the Automatically Update Document Styles command

This command tells Word to automatically change all the styles in the document to match those in the template whenever the document is opened.

---

### *Warning*

You do not want to select this if you have applied local formatting in the document.

---

### To modify all occurrences of a style in the document

First, be sure this is what you want to do. Save a version of the file to another directory before doing this.

1. Place your cursor on an element with the style you want to change.
2. Select Format-Style. The style will be checked in the list.
3. Select Modify.
4. Modify the style as you wish.
5. Select Apply.

Use the Undo button to reverse this action if you need to. If you can't reverse it, restore the file from your backup.

### To save style changes to the template

To store the changes to a style that you made while working in a chapter to the template, follow these steps.

Changes to the template will not automatically be reflected in other files unless you have checked the Automatically Update Document Styles box in File-Templates in each document.

1. Place your cursor on an element with the style you want to change.
2. Select Format-Style. The style will be checked in the list.
3. Select Modify.
4. Modify the style as you wish.
5. In the bottom left corner of the Modify Style dialog box is the check box Add to Template. Check this before you leave this dialog box.
6. Select Apply.

### To update selected styles

If you change the styles in one chapter, and do not have the Automatically Update Document Styles box checked, you can still add the changed style to individual chapters when you'd like.

1. Select Format-Style.
2. Select Organizer.

3. Copy the changed style into this document. Copy it from either the template, if you saved the updated style there, or from the chapter in which you made the style change.

### Text styles

To print out all the styles used in a document, select File-Print. In the Print What list box, select Styles.

**Body Text** is Times New Roman, 12 points. Body text is used for the explanation of the guideline.

**List** style is built off of Body Text. It uses the same font and size as Body text, but it will place a bullet and the proper tabbed space (.2 inch) before your paragraph. Bullets are aligned with the body text. Only one level of bullet is used.

These styles are designed for optimum online viewing. A suggestion to increase paper usability, if you are creating only a paper document, is to make a new style for the first bullet and make it have the same space above as Body Text.

Numbered lists are also currently tagged with List style. You may want to create a new style for numbered lists so that you can control their appearance separately from the bullet style. You may also want to make a new style for the first item in a numbered list.

**Example** style is applied to text examples. It is usually Body Text indented. Some examples are hand formatted.

## Section Breaks

Each guideline chapter is in its own section, separated by section breaks. Do not delete these section breaks.

## Headers and Footers

### Headers

No running headers are used in these documents.

## Footers

For usability, the footers are designed to print the title and first level headings (chapter titles). This way readers immediately can see where they are in the book.

1. You can change the footers by going to View-Header and Footer. Click on the header/footer toggle icon.

**Header/Footer toggle**

2. If you see normal words in the footer, place your cursor in one of them. Press the right mouse button and select Toggle Field Codes.

```
  Even Page Footer -Section 3-
{PAGE}  {SYMBOL 183 \f "Symbol"}  {styleref "heading 1"} - {Title}
```

Be sure you understand what the field is doing before you alter or delete it. Once you understand the field code, make any alterations you need.

---

### *Hint*

To change the Title field, go to File-Summary Info and enter the new title into the Title field in the dialog box.

---

## *Pagination*

Page numbering is set to flow automatically from one chapter to another, starting each chapter on an odd page. There are no section numbers. Instead the title and the chapter name (the first level heading), appear in each footer.

This way if you add or delete pages early in the book the page numbers will adjust throughout. However, it means that you may have to reprint much of the book when you change pagination.

Page numbers are on the outside margin and are contained in the footer.

Be sure you understand how page numbering works with multifile books if you break the file into separate files by chapter.

## Master Document Feature

Word 6.0a has a new feature for building books called *Master Document.* At this time this feature takes a long time to work, and uses a great deal of memory in its operation. For these reasons it is suggested that if you break the document into chapter files you use RD codes rather than with the Master Document feature to link the files together for indexing and a table of contents.

## Checkmarks

You may want to move the checkmarks to the beginning of the guideline text. This makes more sense for a paper document.

One method to do this is:

1. Create a two-celled table without borders.
2. Size the table so that the left cell is in the white space to the left of the text and the guideline text, when placed in the right cell, lines up with the other text.
3. Move the checkmark to the left cell.
4. Enlarge the checkmark.
5. Adjust the space above the checkmark so it works correctly with the guideline text. Give it its own style.
6. Select the table and checkmark and save it as an Auto-Text item. (Edit-Auto Text)

7. Insert the Auto-Text item before each guideline and move the guideline text into the right cell.

8. Eliminate any extra hard returns.

9. Repeat steps 7 and 8 for each required guideline.

### Section headings

Most chapters have two or more content sections to divide the guidelines into groups, helping the reader to understand, retain, and find the information.

These are all formatted in Heading 2 style.

## Tables of Contents and Other Automatic Lists

The published version of the guidelines contains the following lists:

❏ The book table of contents

❏ Chapter tables of contents, first page in each chapter

❏ List of guidelines at the end of each chapter

❏ List of Guidelines chapter following all subject-matter chapters

All of these except the book-level table of contents have been removed from the text file you received because they are not needed online. You can re-create these in your paper document, but it will require an advanced knowledge of Word and significant effort. A few pointers follow.

### Book table of contents

This page currently lists only the level one headings for a table of contents. If you wish to put a more detailed table of contents here, look at the field code. Change the 1-1 to 1-2 or 1-3, depending on how much detail you want to include.

If you add or delete chapters you will need to refresh this list.

1. Place your cursor inside the table of contents field.

2. Press F9.

---

> ### Note
>
> If you have divided the file into chapter files, you need to create a separate file for the table of contents and index. Place RD codes listing each chapter in this file and create a table of contents field and an index field beneath the list by using Insert-Index and Tables and your choices.
>
> Example of an RD code:  `{ RD·introduc.doc }`

Place section breaks after the list of RD codes and between the table of contents and the index. Set the pagination for each section.

Be sure all your files are all in the same directory and that when you do File-Open the directory is set to the directory holding all the files.

### Chapter-level tables of contents

A very usable way to design books is to have a short table of contents at the beginning, containing only chapter titles, and then have detailed tables of contents in each chapter. However, this will require a separate file for each chapter and a sophisticated Word user to create and maintain this feature.

The easiest thing to do is to create a more detailed table of contents for the beginning of the book.

### Lists of guidelines in chapters

This section refers to the List of guidelines for a chapter which appears at the end of each chapter. Users requested this list and have found it helpful. However, it will be difficult to create and maintain unless you have broken the large file up into chapter-files.

These lists are also created with the Insert-Index and Tables feature. For this list pick only second and third level headings.

### List of Guidelines chapter

This chapter is a listing of all the guidelines, by chapter and section, with page numbers. It is not included in your file, you will have to make it.

You should break up the large file into chapter-level files if you are going to create this chapter. Use RD codes in a new file to call all the other files.

The table of contents code for generating this list is:

{·TOC·\o·"1-3"·}¶

### Index

The index file is created just like the Table of Contents file or the List of Guidelines chapter. First create an RD code list of all chapters, then use Insert-Index and Tables to create the index itself.

## *The indexing process*

The index in this file has been optimized for online use. You should test it with paper users before doing any work on it. Use the results of your testing to add, change, or delete tags. Because of the structure of online keyword search, many tags are kept at a more general level than is optimum for a paper index.

Indexing takes two separate operations. First you must place, in each file, the codes indicating that a given term should be included in the index. Consult the Word manual if you are unfamiliar with this process. Second, you must generate the index.

Since Word's master document feature uses a great deal of memory, we suggest you use RD field codes to set up the index. See the manual for further information.

### Marking index entries

Index each topic in a multiple ways, trying to anticipate how users will want to look up the information.

Do not rely on the guideline titles as index entries, as they are not phrased in a useful way for indexing.

### Updating the index list

Before building the index list, check the following:

- ❏ Close all applications except Word.
- ❏ Optional but suggested: If you have been working for a while, close out of Word and Windows and restart. This clears the memory.

If you have divided the file into subfiles, also do the following:

- ❏ Be sure that when you select File-Open the directory is set to the directory that holds all the files.
- ❏ Close all files except your index file.

Update the index

1. Position the cursor in the index field.
2. Press F9.

### Page and column breaks

Review the printout out, or review the file in Page Layout view online. If the columns and pages break at awkward places, insert either a column or page break to force a more usable break.

### Proofing the index list

Look over the list of indexed items for these problems:

- ❏ Multiple-indexed terms due to inconsistency in plural/singular forms, tense, and misspelling
- ❏ Uninformative and general terms
- ❏ Awkward column and page breaks

Do a usability test. Ask someone to look at five to ten pages and identify how they would look up the information. Then have them see if the information is indexed the way they would want to look it up.

## Graphics

### Checkmark icon

The checkmark icon is used for required guidelines.

It is a bitmapped image. It is placed as a picture (Edit-Paste Special-Picture). For usability on paper you may want to enlarge it and move it to before the guideline phrase.

### Screen shots

The screen shots are bitmapped images placed as pictures. It is very important that you place them as pictures rather than linked or embedded objects because pictures take up the least file space. (Wextech makes a product named Quicture which can help you with the size of the file or files.)

To place graphics as pictures

1. Highlight the graphic, either in Word or in the draw or paint application.
2. Select Edit-Copy.
3. If you are in a draw or paint application, switch to Word and highlight the graphic to be replaced.
4. Select Edit-Paste Special.
5. Click Picture.

The graphic will be placed as a picture. You can confirm this by looking at the micro-line help at the bottom of the screen. It will say "Double-click to edit."

To edit the graphic, copy it and paste it into Paintbrush or a similar program. Then repeat the above steps to replace it in your file.

### Scaling graphics

You can scale bitmaps from within Word by highlighting the graphic and then grabbing a corner with the mouse. Slide the mouse in or out. Watch the micro-line help to see the percentage of change you are creating.

The scaled graphic will not look nice onscreen but it will probably print clearly. Check a printout to verify this. (Do not scale graphics in Word if the file is going to become online help.)

### Alignment of screen shots and callouts

For the paper document, align the left edge of the screen image with the text. Allow the callouts to appear in the left margin.

### Placing callouts on images

Word has a handy feature in its draw package for placing callouts on images. You can do this directly in Word, or you can double-click on the image, which opens the Word draw program, and place them there. The advantage of placing the callouts in the draw package is that when you return the image to Word, the captions are part of the graphic and will not be lost if you move the graphic.

To place callouts using Word's draw package:

1. Double-click on the image. Be sure MS Word draw program is activated.
2. Click on this icon in the draw toolbar:
3. Click the mouse when the pointer is where you want the line from the image to the callout to start. Drag the mouse to where you want the caption.
4. Type the caption.
5. Format the text.
6. Format the caption, line, and box by using the other tools on the toolbar.

### Removing callouts from images

Be sure you remove both the lines and box for the callout, even if they are not displayed, as well as the text. Click on the edge of the text border, then press Delete.

## Tables

Study the table feature in Word so you understand how easy it is to work with tables. Change the style of the tables (optimized for online) to a more attractive appearance for paper.

## Printing

### Before printing

Before printing you will want to do a few things.

- ❑ Do a spell check of all files you have changed.
- ❑ Check page breaks online. Use manual page breaks to avoid breaking a guideline across pages.
- ❑ Make sure each chapter begins with an odd page and ends with an even page.
- ❑ If you are using multiple files, check pagination of chapters in order, making sure each chapter starts with the next odd page.
- ❑ If you are using them, rebuild the lists of guidelines at the end of the chapters and the chapter called *List of Guidelines*.
- ❑ Rebuild the index and the master table of contents.

### Printing an individual chapter

If you are using one file, enter the section command in the Print dialog box. See Word's help topic *Setting printing options* for help.

If you are using multiple files, open a chapter and print it as you would any other file.

### Printing the entire manual

If you are using one file, print it as you would any other file. This is a very large file with many graphics. It may take hours to print, depending on the speed and memory of your printer. You may want to print it in sections.

If you are using multiple files, the safest way to print the book is to print each chapter in order, checking the pagination of each chapter as printed. That way, if your pagination is off early in the book, you can correct the error before you have printed a large volume of paper.

You can print all the files at once by using Find File. The files will not print in book order, so you will have to reorganize them after printing them. To print this way:

1. Select File-Find File. Click on Search.
2. In the File Name list box, type *.DOC.
3. In the Location list box, type the directory path and name.
4. Highlight the files you want to print.
5. Select Commands-Print.

If you do not understand how to use Find File, refer to online help or a manual.

### Screen shot quality

If you are distributing paper output and the screen images print too dark on your printer, try printing on a different printer or adjusting the resolution of your printer.

If these remedies do not work, copy and paste the graphics into Paintbrush or a similar bitmap paint program and replace the gray tones with a lighter gray or white.

### Check the printout before duplicating

Check your printout carefully before you duplicate it or send it to a printer. Check for:

- ❑ Page breaks
- ❑ Page numbers
- ❑ Footers correctly formatted
- ❑ Graphics and captions correctly placed
- ❑ Headings and text have correct styles applied
- ❑ Checkmark lined up with text correctly

# From Paper to Online

## Introduction

This section covers special tasks if you are delivering both a paper version of the guidelines and an online from a single file. Be sure to read the *Online Help* section.

You will need to use Doc-To-Help.

## Initial Process

1. Make your text changes in the .DOC file (or files). Use Doc-To-Help to break the file into smaller files if you are going to do this. Follow Doc-To-Help's instructions.
2. Make changes in the paper document.
3. Do not add or apply new styles unless you understand the Doc-To-Help templates. (You will need to change the styles in two templates, one for paper and one for online.)
4. Add or change keywords (indexed terms).
5. Create a Glossary if you want one.

## Make into Help

You must divide the process of turning the .DOC file or files into help into a two step process. Otherwise you will probably get Out of Memory messages.

1. Check only the first and second boxes in the dialog box Reformat as Help File.
2. In the .RTF file, check the remaining boxes one at a time.
3. Do not compile yet.

### Screen Shot Alignment

In the .DOC file as distributed with these materials, the screen shots are lined up so that they will look good printed on paper. You will need to change all these hand-applied alignments to straighten Body Text.

1. Select Edit-Replace.
2. In the Find What box, enter no text but select Body Text for formatting.
3. In the Replace With box, do the same—enter no text but select Body Text for formatting.
4. Select Replace All.

### Bullets

Check the bullets and correct if necessary.

1. Search on the style List.
2. Make sure each List style (bullet list, not numbered) has one bullet.
3. Make sure each List style, numbered, does not have any bullets.

### Add the Navigator

If you have changed the order of any topics or added or deleted topics, you will need to refresh the topic list in the Navigator. Follow Doc-To-Help's instructions.

# Index

Screen images (*continued*)
   color, 140
   creating, 156
   customize, 153
   in online help, 139
   modify, 140
   monochrome, 140
   scaling, 140
Scrolling
   avoiding, 40, 143
   horizontal, 40
   menus, 54
   multiple-select list box, 24
   regions in help, 123
Secondary windows
   buttons, 128
   definitions, 122
   in help, 121
   sizing, 42
Select all
   buttons, 24
   check boxes, 19
Separator bars, 55
Shading in help, 145
Size
   data fields, 33
   files, 141
   fonts, 97, 144
   help windows, 143
   menu bar, 53
   secondary windows, 42
   windows, 122
Sliders
   arrows, 27
   data entry, 27
   results, 26
   using, 25, 26
Spin boxes, 25
Standards, 4
   committee, 160
   icons, 82
Subscript/Superscript
   creating in help, 145
Symbol
   cascading menu, 55
   information, 64
   warnings, 65
System errors, 66

**T**

Tables
   borders in help, 145
   online help, 145

   using, 104
   Windows compiler, 145
Task force coordinator, 156
Tasks
   ordering information, 44
   windows, 43
Testing
   color, 142
   help, 143
   icons, 82
   index, 138
   menus, 50, 52
   metaphors, 92
Text
   colors, 74, 75, 96
   fonts, 96
Tiling, windows, 40
   Toggling, toolbars, 85
Toolbars
   active items, 85
   consistency, 85
   graying out, 85
   menu items, 84
   moving, 85
   multiple, 85
   placement, 85
   toggling, 85
   using, 84
Topic titles
   capitalization, 144
   help contents, 125
   indexing, 134, 137, 138
   types, 125
   Translation, icons, 81
   Typefaces. *See* Fonts

**U**

Underlining
   emphasis, 145
   readability, 96
   redundant cueing, 142
Updating
   guidelines, 161, 162
   guidelines manual, 161
Usability
   graphics, 140
   graphing, 104
   indexing, 136
   messages, 62
   online help, 116
   readability. *See* Readability
   testing, references, 4
Users

   first draft, 157
   roll-out plan, 159

**V**

Version control
   online help, 116
Versions. *See* Revision dates
Visual coding
   attention, 100, 101
   blinking, 101
   bolding, 101
   emphasis, 101
   reverse video, 100
   using, 100
Voice
   messages, 63
   online help, 119

**W**

Waiting time, 69
Warnings
   messages, 65
   symbols, 65
White space
   grouping, 86
   grouping data, 45
   push buttons, 6
   readability, 126
Windows
   cascading, 40
   flow, 46
   grouping data, 45
   organizing, 43
   presentation, 40
   sizing secondary, 42
   tiling, 40
   types, 122
Wording
   acronyms, 64
   menu items, 50, 53
   menus, 54
   messages, 64
   online help, 126
Work flow
   analysis, references, 2
   matching to system flow, 110
   ordering information, 44
   organizing windows, 43
   tasks, 43

# INSTANT GUI STANDARDS FOR YOUR COMPANY!

This complete book is available on CD in Windows Help files. Use these guidelines as a foundation for your own corporate GUI standards. Add to them, customize them, make them your *own*. Appendix C in this book is your documentation and shows you how to install the software. To order, mail this card in, or fax it to (212) 850-6264, or email your request to compbks@jwiley.com.

---

☐ **Single-User CD Only**
Please send me _____ copy(ies) of the single-user version of *Guidelines for Enterprise-Wide GUI Design Single-User CD Only* at $65.00 each. Order #471-12633-0.

☐ **Site License CD Only**
Please send me _____ copy(ies) of the worldwide site license CD only for *Guidelines for Enterprise-Wide GUI Design Site License CD Only* at $1,265.00 each. Order #471-12632-2.

☐ **Book Only**
Please send me _____ copy(ies) of the book *Guidelines for Enterprise-Wide GUI Design* at $29.95 each. Weinschenk/GUI Guide, order #471-11845-1.

☐ Visa    ☐ MasterCard    ☐ American Express    ☐ Check

CARD# _____ EXP. DATE _____

NAME _____ SIGNATURE _____

COMPANY _____

STREET _____ _____

CITY/STATE _____ ZIP CODE _____

TELEPHONE # _____ EMAIL _____

## BUSINESS REPLY MAIL
FIRST CLASS    PERMIT NO. 2277    NEW YORK, N.Y.

POSTAGE WILL BE PAID BY ADDRESSEE

**JOHN WILEY & SONS, INC.**
**Attn: Ellen Reavis**
**605 Third Avenue, 10th floor**
**New York, N.Y. 10158-0012**